Dedicated to Savy and Peanut, who make every day an adventure. Thank you for traveling the world with us.

EGYPT

⊖

Educational Resources, Crafts & Activities for Kids

Sarah M. Prowant, MSN-Ed, RN

Savy Activities
Colorado, USA

TERMS & CONDITIONS

FOR BEST RESULTS:

When assembling a 3D model, glue a second piece of thick paper with a craft glue stick to back of each sheet of model pieces (prior to cutting pieces) to provide additional stability when assembled.

Laminate all cards & posters with at least 3 ml lamination for additional protection.

If printing from an ebook, cardstock paper (>60 lbs) provides best results for cards, models and manipulative activities, while standard printer paper is adequate for recipes, lessons, etc. Please set printer to "FIT TO PAGE" when printing for best results.

FOLLOW US ON SOCIAL MEDIA!

@savyactivities

/SavyActivities

www.SavyActivities.com

WHATS INCLUDED:

- Educational Placemat/Poster & Flag
- Egypt Landmark Three-Part Cards
- Egypt Landmark & Cities Map Pinning
- Egypt Continent Flag Pinning & Outline
- Egypt Fauna Three-Part Cards
- Egypt Fun Facts
- Egyptian History Timeline Poster
- Ancient Egyptian Calendar
- 3D Giza Plateau Model w/Pyramid Design Cards
- Ancient Egyptian Paper Dolls
- Apple Mummification Experiment
- Sarcophagus Model & Canopic Jar Matching
- Toilet Paper Mummy
- Egyptian Gods Info Cards
- Sundial Craft
- Senet Game
- Papyrus Making
- Hieroglyphic Code Card Matching
- *Tale of the Doomed Prince* Minibook
- Ancient Egyptian Music Poster
- Egyptian Pound Currency
- Units of Measurement (World Landmarks)
- Life Cycle Spinner - Egyptian Mau
- Khayamiya Fabric Craft
- Steppe Eagle Craft
- Fez Hat Craft
- Fanous Lantern
- Pillars of Islam Craft
- Hamsa Hand Incense Burner
- Cotton Craft w/Flashcards
- Ful Medames Recipe
- Sahara Desert Habitat Matching
- Kolla Pottery Painting & Matching Cards
- Egyptian Arabic Language Cards

Egypt

National Flora: Lotus

National Fauna: Steppe Eagle

Capital City: Cairo

Currency: Egyptian Pound LE

Language: Arabic

National Holiday(s): July 23

Famous Landmarks:

Great Pyramids
Great Sphyinx
Abu Simbel Temple
Valley of the Kings
Nile River
Luxor Temple
Karnak Temple
Colossi of Memnon
St. Catherine's Monastery
White Desert

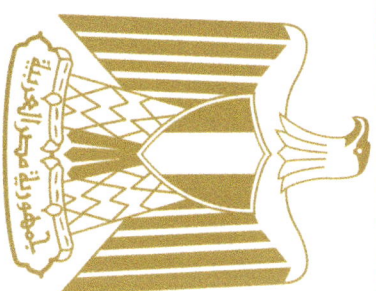

Egypt

Egypt Landmarks (3-Part Cards)

Great Sphinx

Great Pyramids

Abu Simbel Temple

Valley of the Kings

Egypt Landmarks (3-Part Cards)

Great Sphinx

Great Pyramids

Abu Simbel Temple

Valley of the Kings

Egypt Landmarks (3-Part Cards)

Nile River

Luxor Temple

Karnak Temple

Colossi of Memnon

Egypt Landmarks (3-Part Cards)

Nile River

Luxor Temple

Karnak Temple

Colossi of Memnon

Egypt Landmarks (3-Part Cards)

St. Catherine's Monastery

St. Catherine's Monastery

White Desert

White Desert

Egypt Landmarks

Cut out circles using a 1" circle punch or scissors. Place circles on map where the landmarks are located. Refer to the control version for help if needed.

Egypt Cities

Cut out the labels and attach them to the diagram

Cairo	Alexandria	Giza	Luxor
Aswan	Sharm El Sheikh	Hurghada	Port Said
Suez			
Asyut			

Instructions

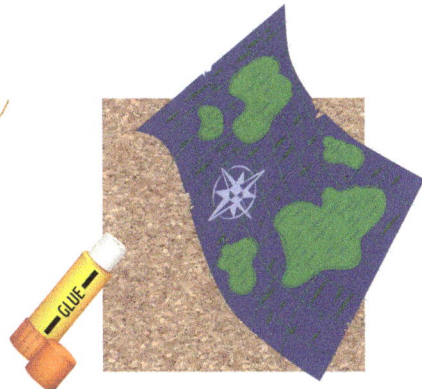

Paste included map illustration onto foamboard, cardboard or corkboard. Glue straight or T-pin to back of labels or photo circles and pin into map at appropriate location of landmark or city.

Egypt

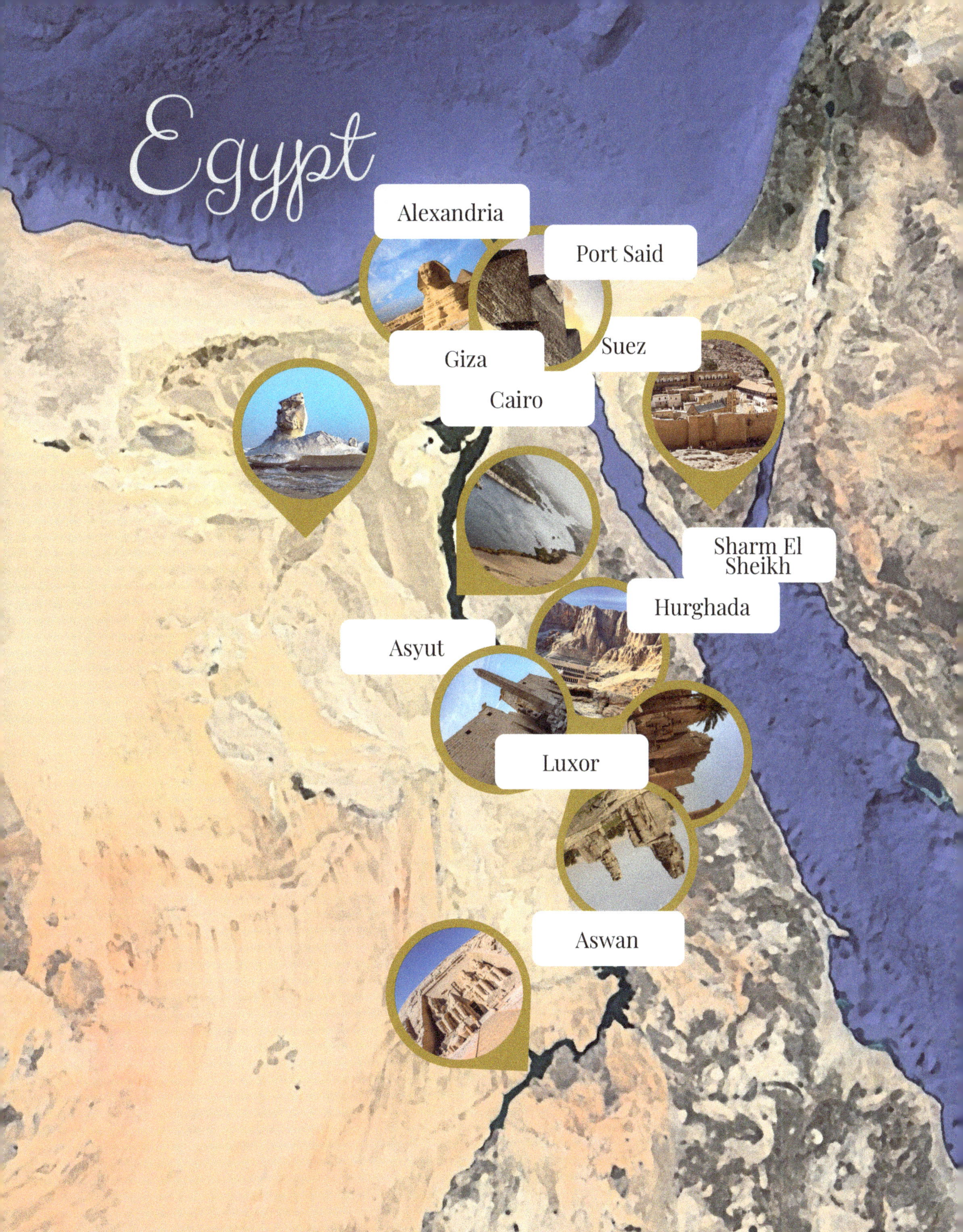

Egypt
Alexandria
Port Said
Giza
Suez
Cairo
Sharm El Sheikh
Hurghada
Asyut
Luxor
Aswan

**Please note that the locations may not be exact as markers are positioned to be seen when multiple locations are in similar area.*

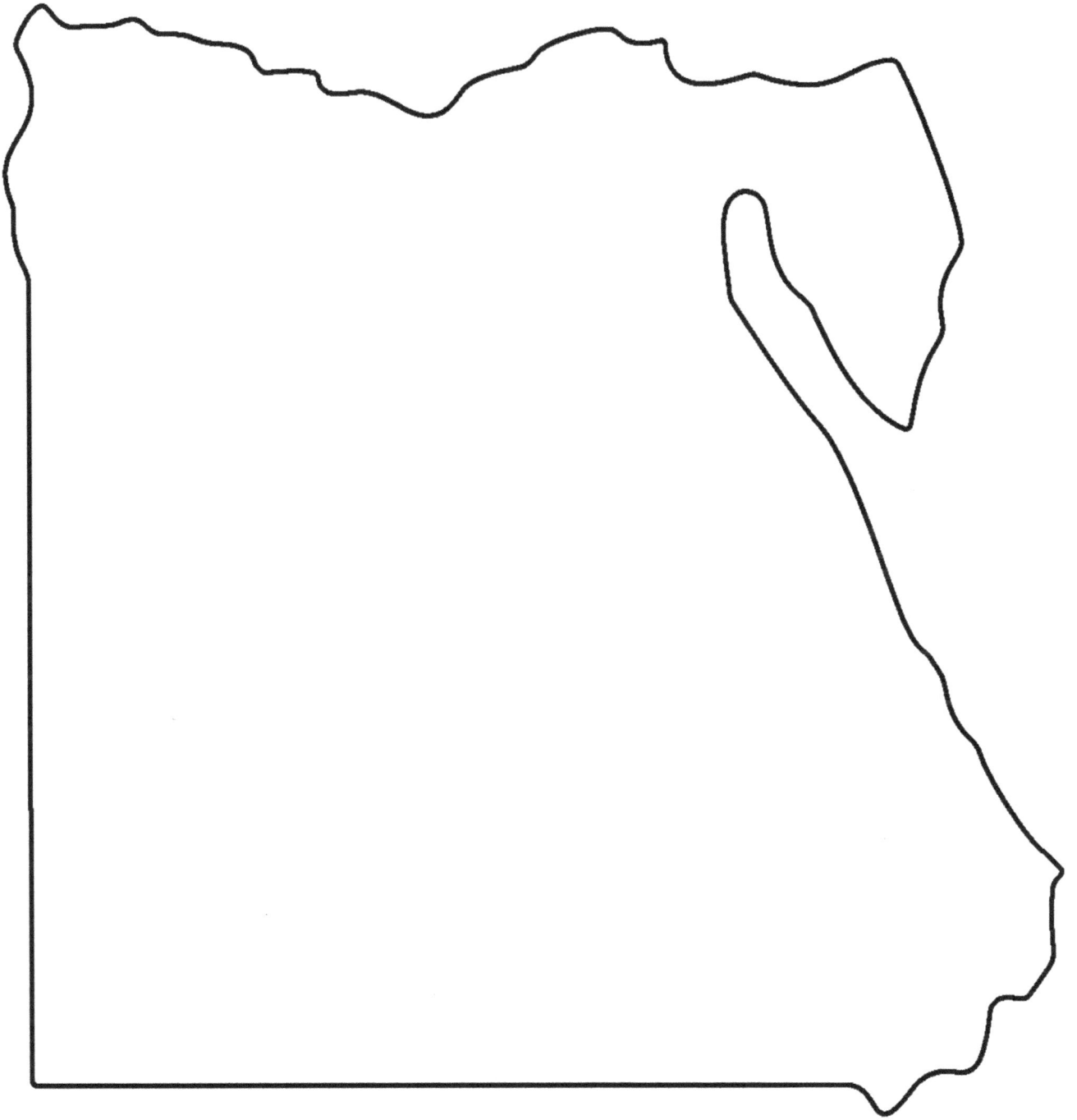

Egypt

Africa Continent: Egypt

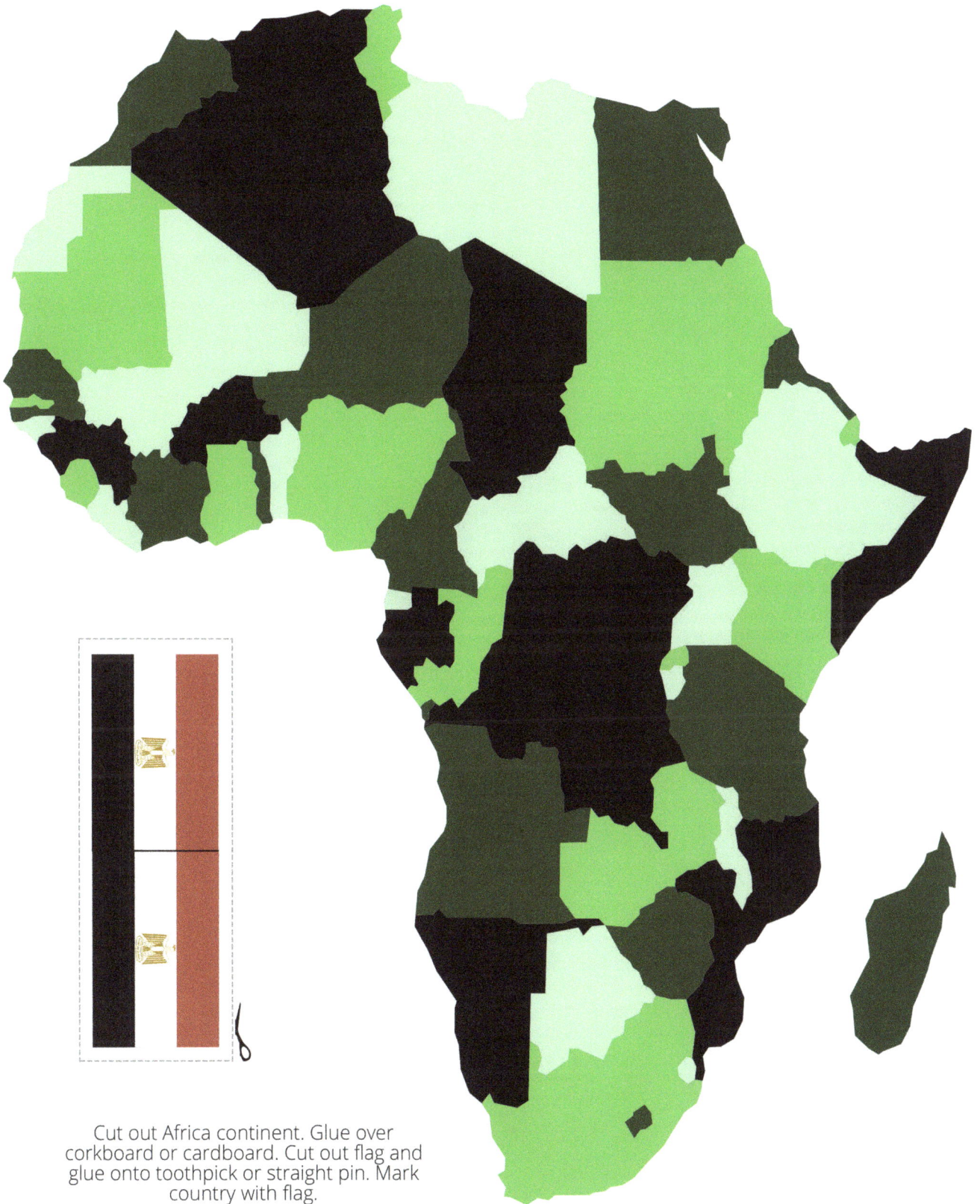

Cut out Africa continent. Glue over corkboard or cardboard. Cut out flag and glue onto toothpick or straight pin. Mark country with flag.

Egypt Fauna (3-Part Cards)

Egyptian Mau

Dromedary Camel

Ibis

Nile Crocodile

Egypt Fauna (3-Part Cards)

Egyptian Mau

Dromedary Camel

Ibis

Nile Crocodile

Egypt Fauna (3-Part Cards)

Egyptian Cobra

Hippopotamus

Lionfish

Steppe Eagle

Egypt Fauna (3-Part Cards)

Egyptian Cobra

Hippopotamus

Lionfish

Steppe Eagle

Egypt Fun Facts

Egypt is known for their two major deserts, the Libyan and the Sahara desert, which cover much of the country's land.

The official name of Egypt is *Junhuriyah Misr al-Arabiya*, meaning "the Arab Republic of Egypt" in English.

With a population of 22 million and measuring 500 square km, Cairo is the largest city in Africa and the Middle East.

Egyptians often relaxed by playing board games, including a game of chance known as "Senet."

The world's oldest dress was found in Egypt, estimated at 5000 years old.

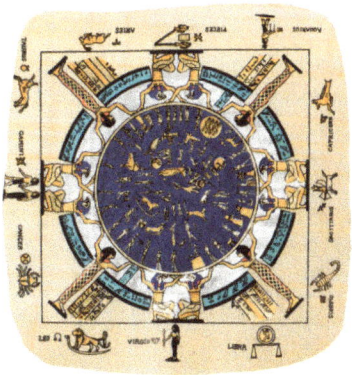

The Ancient Egyptians had so many gods that literally every city had its own favorite deity.

The Egyptians invented the 365-days a year calendar to predict the yearly floodings of the Nile river.

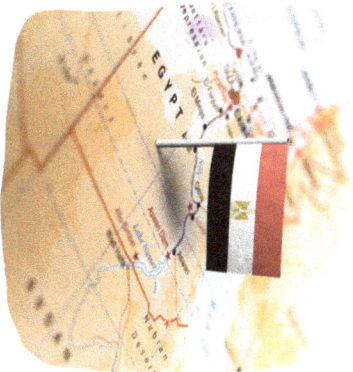

The official language of Egypt is Arabic, making it the largest Arabic population.

Egypt Fun Facts

Cats were considered to be a sacred animal by the Ancient Egyptians, with many homes having them as pets.

Islam is the common religion of Egypt, with 90% of the population being Muslims.

Both men and women in Ancient Egypt wore copious amounts of dark makeup, known as kohl.

The second longest river in the world is the River Nile, which spans over 4,100 miles and flows through many African countries.

The only example of the seven ancient wonders of the world is the Great Pyramid of Khufu, located in Giza.

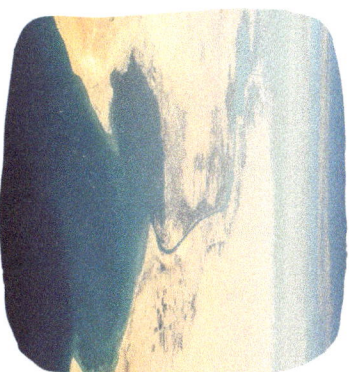

Cleopatra was technically not Egyptian. Although born in Egypt, she was a descendant of a long line of Greek Macedonians.

Egypt borders both the Mediterranean and the Red Sea, with the Suez Canal allowing ships to easily sail between Asia and Europe.

Hieroglyphs, the ancient language once used by the Egyptians, has about 700 symbols!

Timeline of Egyptian History

3000 BC — Hieroglyphics Invented

2,500 — Pyramids Constructed

1341 — Tutankhamun is Born

1300 — Nefertari is Born

332 — Alexander the Great Conquers Egypt

69 — Cleopatra is born

31 — Rome Conquers Egypt

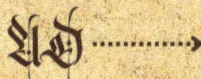

AD

642 — Arabs Conquer Egypt

969 — Cairo Becomes Capital

1517 — Egypt Absorbed into Turkish Ottoman Empire

1859 — Suez Canal Built

1882 — Great Britain Conquers Egypt

1922 — Egypt Gains Independence

Photos used for illustration purposes and may not be of exact event or item.

Ancient Egyptian Calendar

The ancient Egyptian calendar was originally discovered on the ceiling in *Temple of Dendera* in Luxor and estimated to be over 5,000 years old. It is a solar calendar with a 365-day year, consisting of three seasons of 120 days each, with each season divided into four months of 30 days.

GIZA PLATEAU MODEL

Instructions

The Giza Plateau is a plateau in Giza, on the outskirts of Cairo, Egypt, which includes the Great Pyramids of Khufu, Khafre and Menkaure and the Sphinx. It is one of the most recognizable locations in the world, and the largest pyramid (Khufu) is known as one of the seven wonders of the ancient world. Cut out included Giza Plateau model templates. Fold each pyramid together and glue as indicated to form pyramid shape. Use clothespins to keep in place until glue dries. Tape can also be used. After assembling sphinx face, glue to sphinx front in indicated area and the top of face extends backwards to form top of entire head. Glue the back of the sphinx head and attach each tab to one another to create secure head shape. Shape sphinx body over half-circle to form body shape and attach to head through back cutout. Glue on sides. Form the feet the same way as the body and attach to front with glue or tape. Arrange pyramids and sphinx on a sheet of cardboard and glue in place. Use included illustration to place in correct orientation. **Optional:** Glue sand onto cardboard at base. *Relative dimensions of structures slightly changed to accommodate crafting.*

Materials

- Giza Plateau Model Templates
- Scissors
- Craft Glue (or Tape)
- Clothespins
- Cardboard Poster
- Sand (optional)

Pyramid of Khufu

N

The Great Pyramid of Giza is the largest Egyptian pyramid and tomb of Fourth Dynasty pharaoh Khufu. Built in the 26th century BC, it is the oldest of the Seven Wonders of the Ancient World, and the only one to remain largely intact.

Pyramid of Khafre

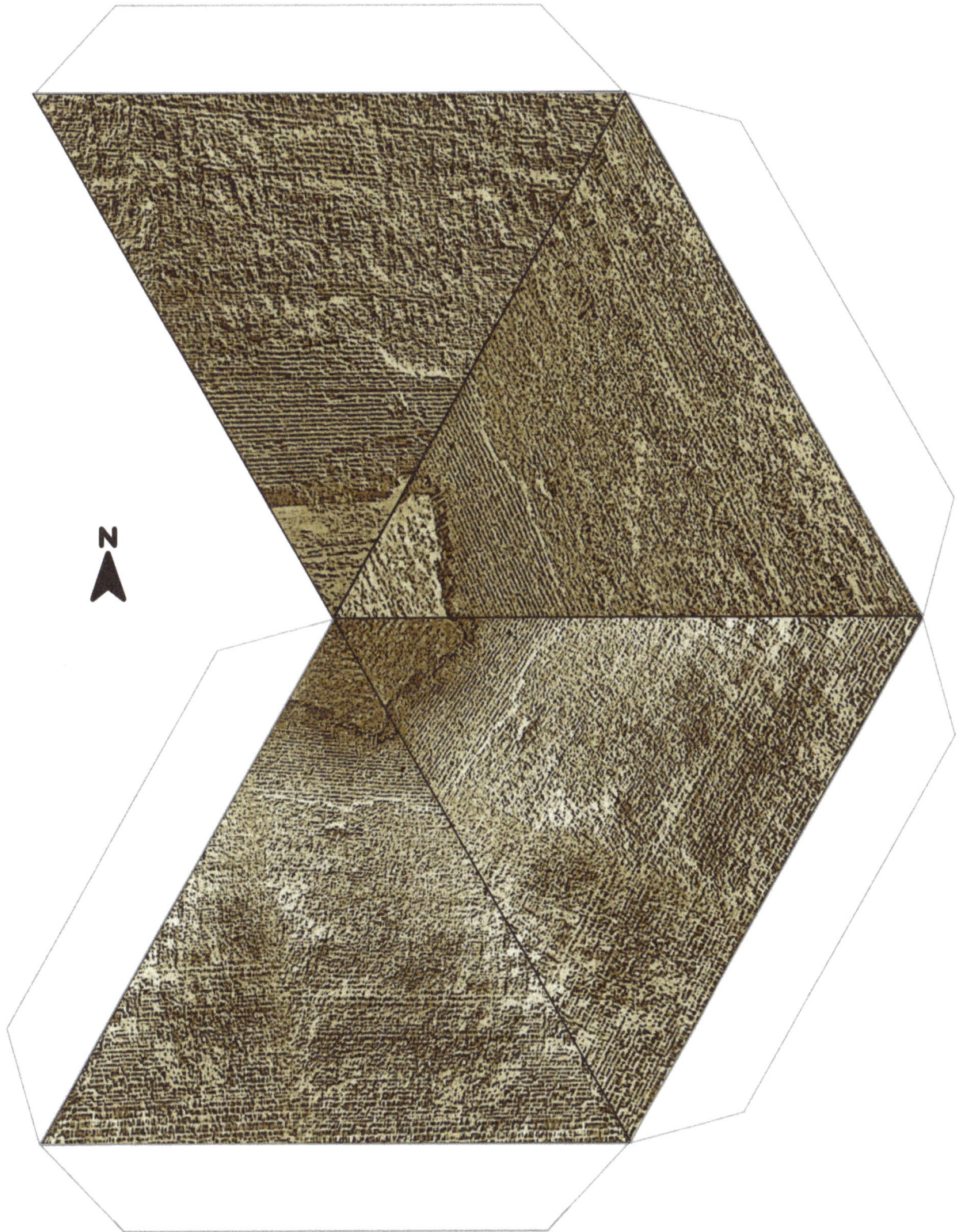

The pyramid of Khafre is the second tallest and second largest of the three ancient Egyptian pyramids of Giza and the tomb of the fourth-dynasty pharaoh, Khafre.

Pyramid of Menkaure

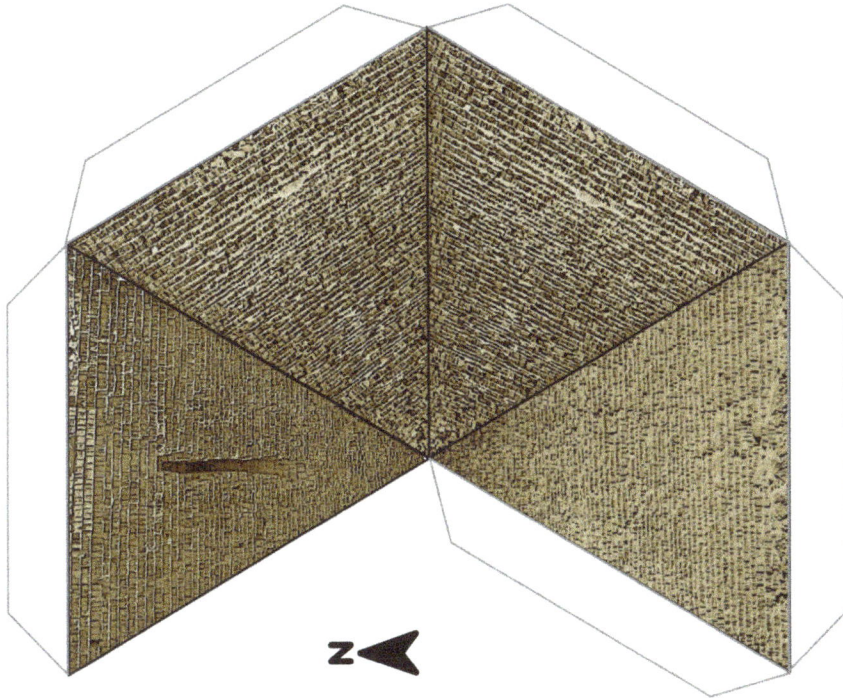

The pyramid of Menkaure is the smallest of the three main Pyramids of Giza, located on the Giza Plateau in the southwestern outskirts of Cairo, Egypt. It is thought to have been built to serve as the tomb of the Fourth Dynasty Egyptian, Pharaoh Menkaure.

Next to both the pyramid of Cheops and Menkaure are three smaller pyramids. It is speculated that the structures were likely tombs for their queens.

G3-A
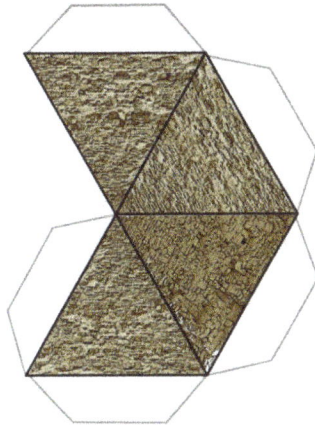

G3-B
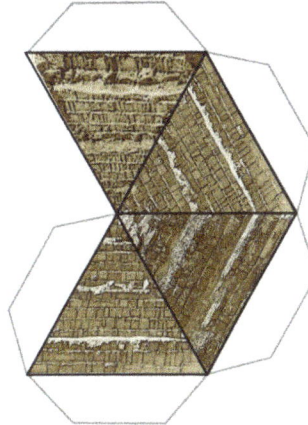

G3-C
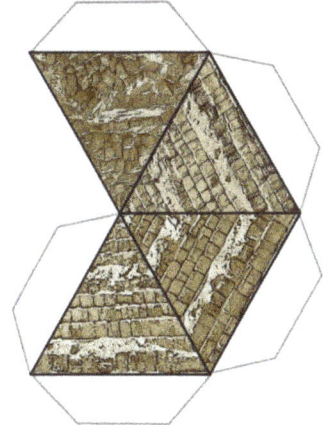

G1-A
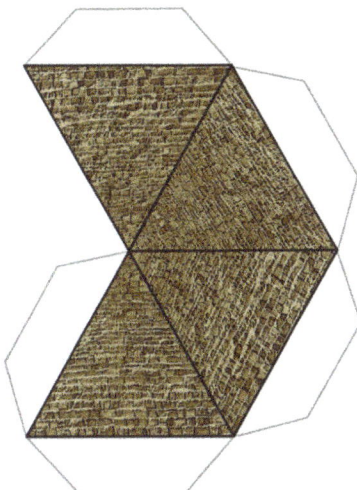

G1-B
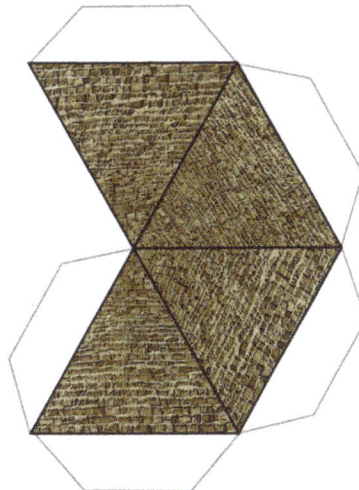

G1-C
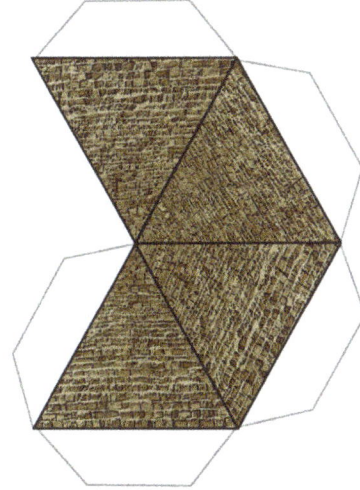

The Great Sphinx

The Great Sphinx of Giza is a statue of a reclining sphinx, a mythical creature with the head of a human, and the body of a lion. It faces directly from west to east, it stands on the Giza Plateau on the west bank of the Nile in Giza, Egypt. The face of the Sphinx appears to represent the pharaoh Khafre. The original shape of the Sphinx was cut from the bedrock and has since been restored with layers of limestone blocks. Its nose was broken off for unknown reasons between the 3rd and 10th centuries AD.

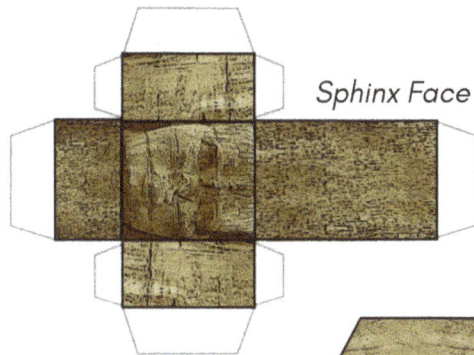

Sphinx Face

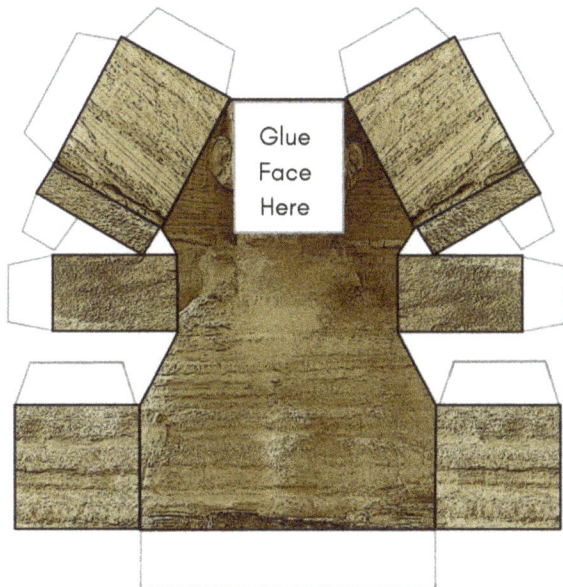

Glue Face Here

Sphinx Head Front

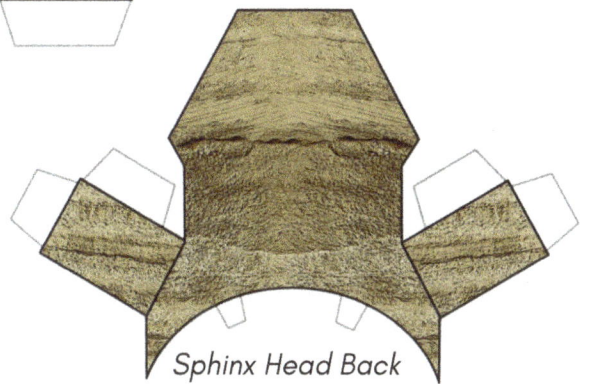

Sphinx Head Back

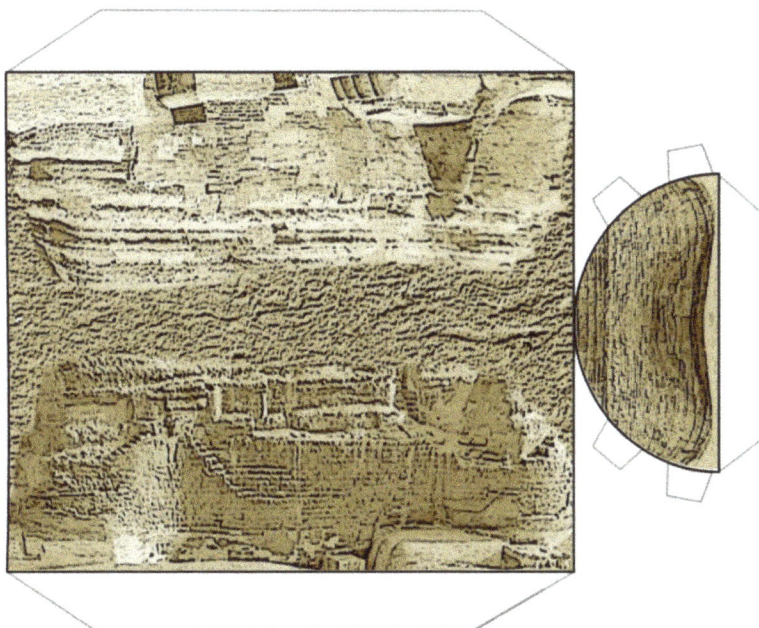

Sphinx Body

Sphinx Legs

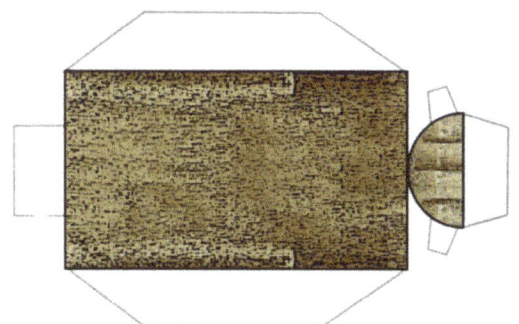

Approximate Positions
Of Monuments

Pyramid of Khafre

Pyramid of Khufu

Pyramid of Menkaure

G1-A

G1-B

G1-C

The Great Sphinx

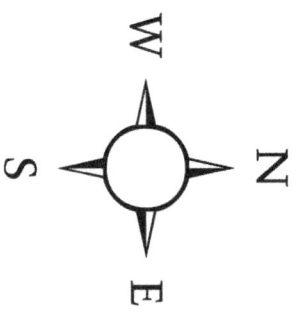

G3-C   G3-B   G3-A

Paper models are different in size ratios, as some re-sizing has been done to allow models to be most usable for educational purposes.

W

N

S

E

Pyramid Passages

Pyramid of Khufu

1 - Original Entrance
2 - Robbers' Tunnel
3 & 4 - Descending Passage
5 - Subterranean Chamber
6 - Ascending Passage
7 - Queen's Chamber & "Air-Shafts"
8 - Horizontal Passage
9 - Grand Gallery
10 - King's Chamber & "Air-Shafts"
11 - Grotto & Well Shaft

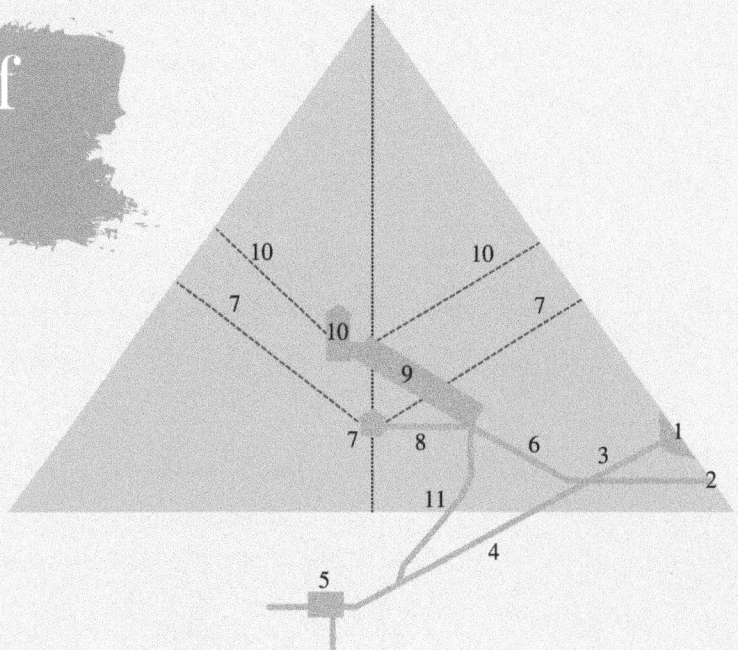

Pyramid of Khafre

1 - Upper Entrance & Passage
2 - Lower Entrance & Passage
3 - Intrusive Tunnel
4 - Lower Burial Chamber
5 - Upper Burial Chamber

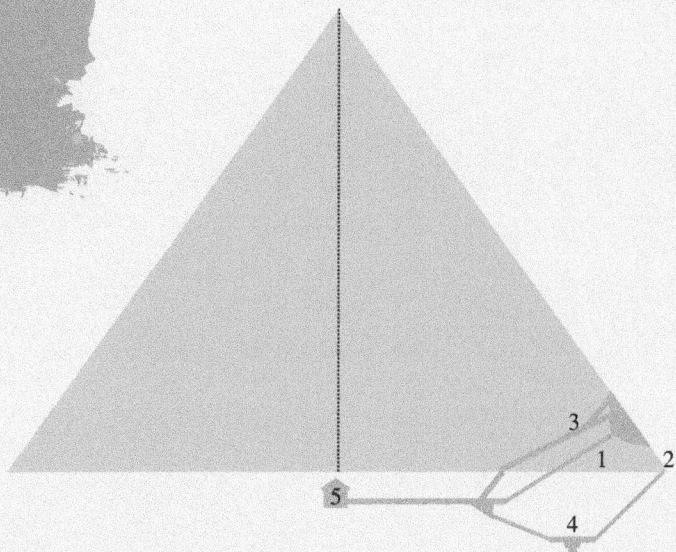

Pyramid Passages

Pyramid of Menkaure

1 – Entrance
2 – Descending Passage
3 – Burial Chambers
4 – Vyse's Tunnel

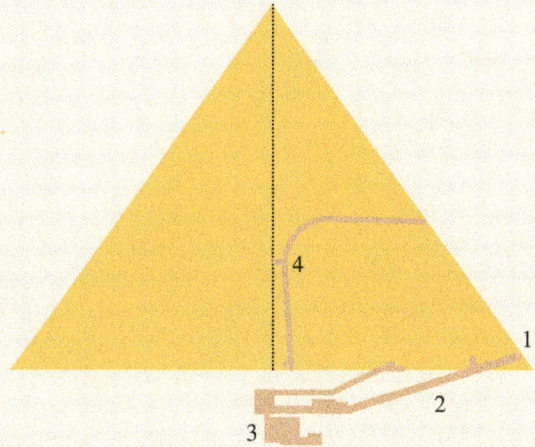

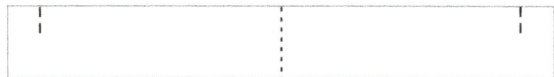

MUMMIFICATION EXPERIMENT

Instructions

Ancient Egyptians believed in the afterlife and attempted to preserve the bodies of those that had died. They used special processes to remove all moisture from the body, leaving only a dried form that would not easily decay. They were so successful that these bodies today are well preserved, even after 3,000 or more years.

Materials
- Apples
- Table Salt
- Baking Soda
- Knife
- Two Containers

In Ancient Egypt, natron was used to preserve mummies. Natron is a natural salt mixture containing the chemicals sodium carbonate, decahydrate (soda ash), sodium bicarbonate (baking soda), sodium chloride (table salt), and another salt called sodium sulfate.

Fill the bottom of one container with salt and add 1-2 Tablespoons baking soda. Cut apples into slices and lay on the bottom of both containers (one with salt and one without salt). Fill the salt container alternating layers of baking soda and salt. The container with just the apples will provide the comparison.

Allow to dry for 1-2 weeks. Compare the apples - which is preserved better? The baking soda and salt mixture preserves the apple's color and shape better than drying naturally.

SACROPHAGUS MODEL

Instructions

In ancient Egypt, mummified bodies were stored in multiple layers of protection. Wealthier Egyptians could afford better burial practices, with Pharaohs and royalty receiving incredible coffins and sarcophaguses. For example, King Tutankhamen's body was stored in three coffins, nested inside one another and finally protected by a large stone sarcophagus. Inner coffins were anthropoid (body shaped) and made of layers of linen or papyrus covered with plaster called cartonnage, or carved out of wood. Often these inner coffins were ornately decorated with paint or gold layers, custom decorated to resemble the features of the deceased.

Cut out included templates. Glue as indicated to form base and covers of the two inner coffins and one outer sarcophagus. Allow to dry thoroughly or use tape. Cut out mummified body and cover with linens, securing with tabs. Place body in smallest coffin (grey) and place in larger anthropoid coffin. Lastly place in stone sarcophagus along with canopic jars, containing the body's internal organs.

Materials

- Sarcophagus Templates
- Scissors
- Tape or Craft Glue

Layers of the Sarcophagus

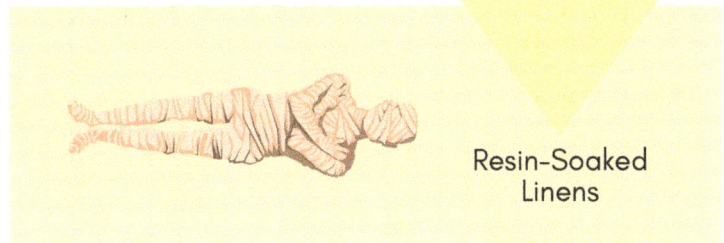

Stone Sarcophagus

Canopic Jars

Anthropoid Wooden Coffin

Cartonnage Case w/Death Mask

Resin-Soaked Linens

Body

Sarcophagus Model

Stone
Sarcophagus –
Base

Canopic Jars

Sarcophagus Model

Stone Sarcophagus - Lid

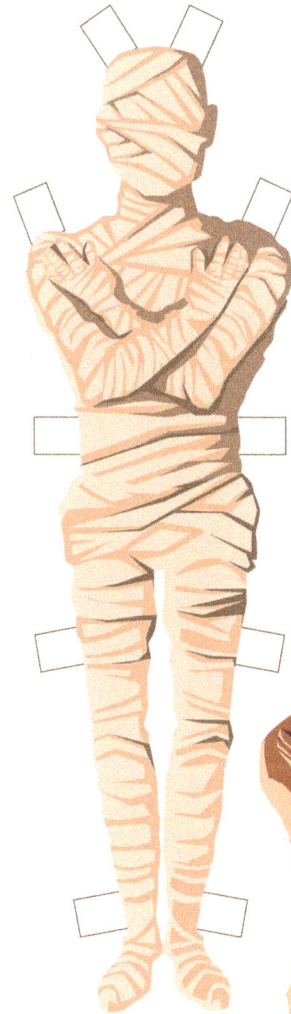

Body

Resin-Soaked
Linens

Sarcophagus Model

Cover

Anthropoid
Wooden Coffin

Base

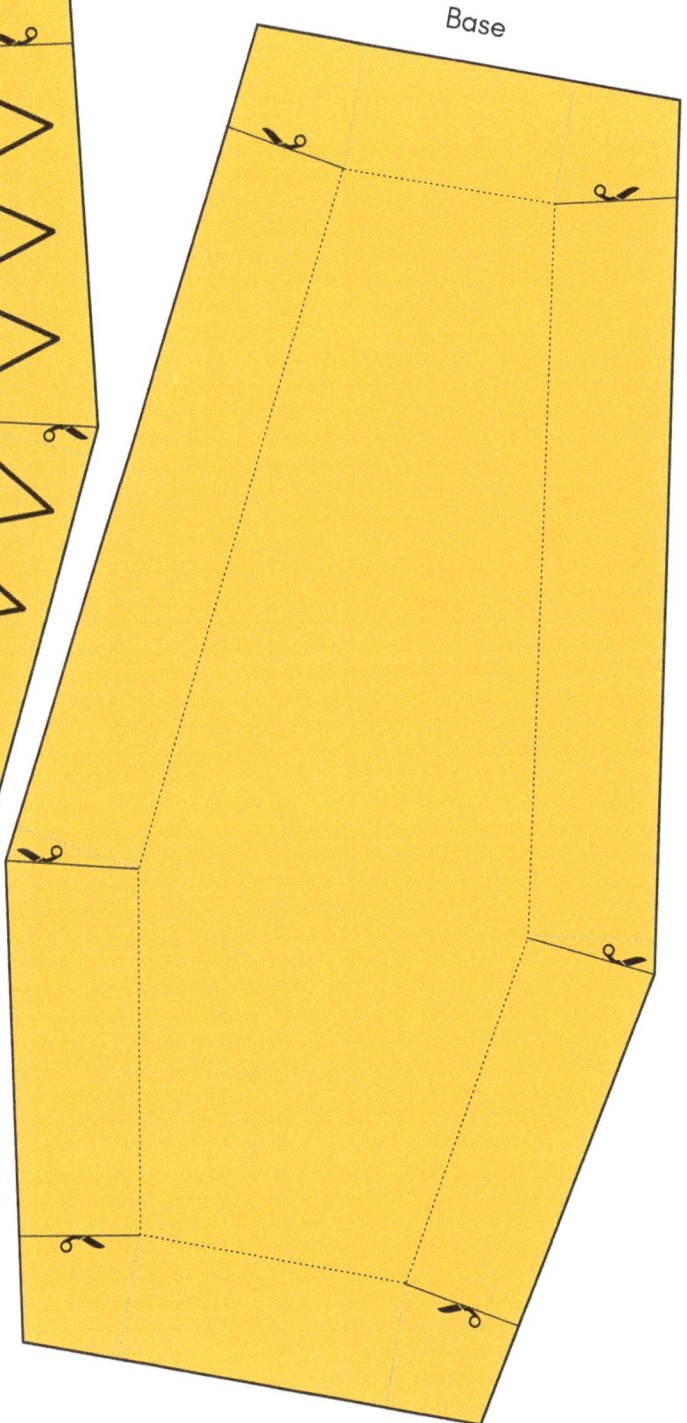

Sarcophagus Model

Cartonnage Case
w/Death Mask

Base

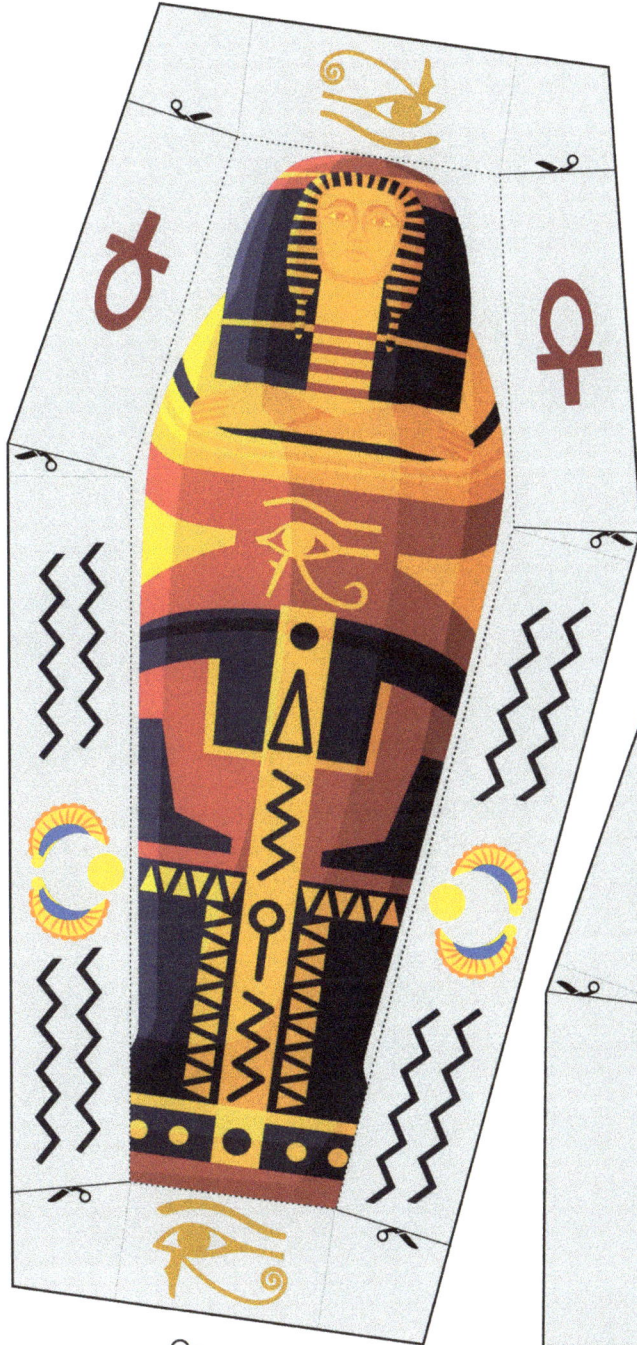

Cover

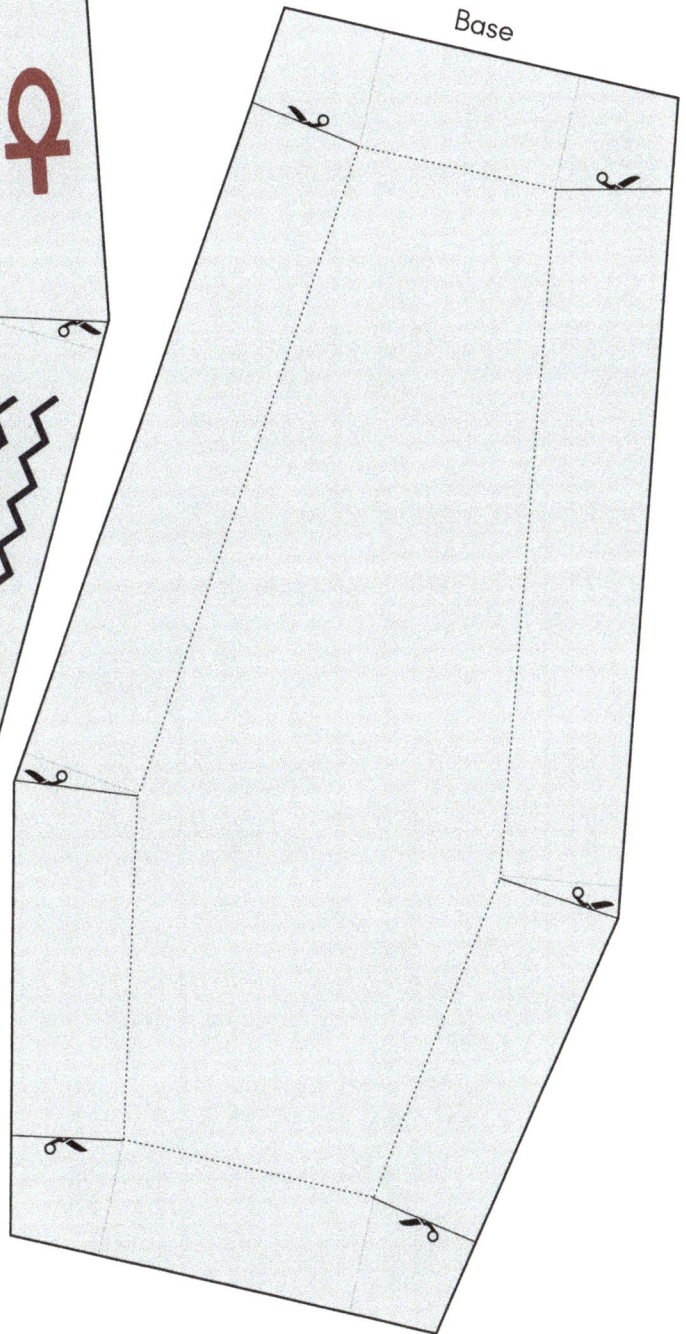

Canopic Jar Matching

Imsety was the human-headed god whose jar contained the liver and was protected by the goddess Isis. **Qebehsenuef** was the falcon-headed god whose jar contained the intestines and was protected by the goddess Serqet. **Hapi** was the baboon-headed god whose jar contained the lungs and was protected by the goddess Nephthys. **Duamutef** was the jackal-headed god whose jar contained the stomach and was protected by the goddess Neith.

Cut out canopic jars - cut out corresponding organs and have child match the correct organ with the correct jar.

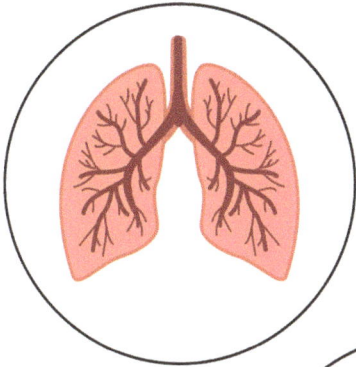

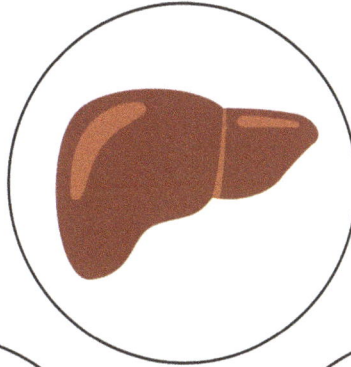

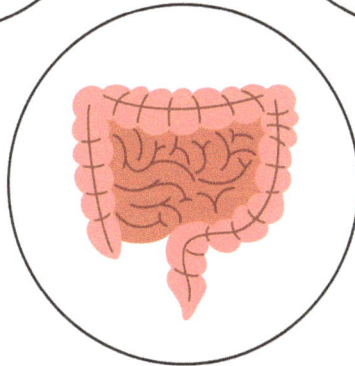

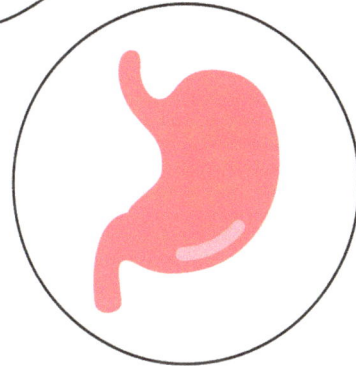

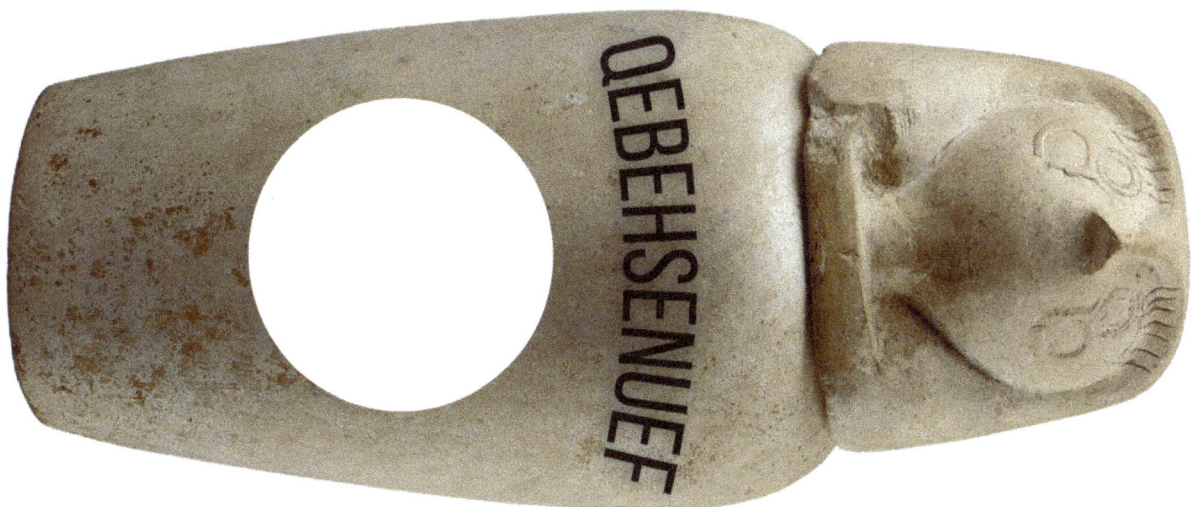

QEBEHSENUEF

Canopic Jar Matching

HAPI

DUAMUTEF

IMSETY

TOILET PAPER MUMMY

Instructions

As part of the mummification process, the body was wrapped in linen (as many as 35 layers) and soaked in resins and oils. This helped preserve the body so well many are still intact thousands of years later.

Give a child roll of toilet paper. Have them carefully wrap another child (or adult) with the paper. Be careful, so the paper doesn't break! Make sure to leave a space for the person to breath!

Once the paper has completely wrapped around the person, consider how many layers there are. Imagine doing this for 35 layers! Discuss trying to do this with a horizontal body that had to be moved for each layer. Don't forget to save the toilet paper for use later!

Materials

- Toilet Paper

Egypt Gods Info Cards

 Bastet

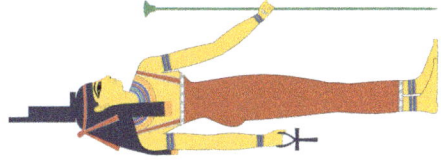 Isis

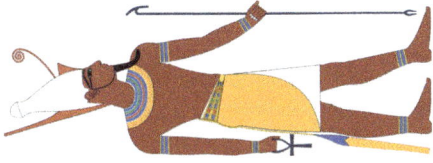 Atum

 Hathor

 Anubis

 Horus

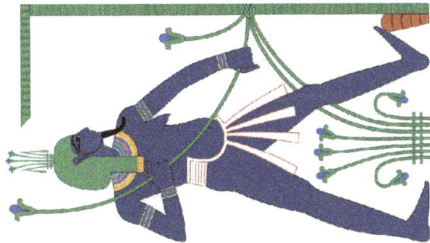 Hapi

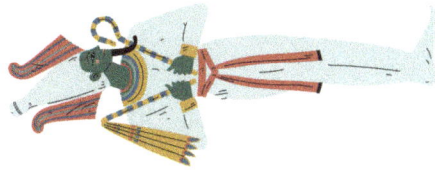 Osiris

Bastet was a cat or lioness warrior goddess of the sun. She was the protector of Lower Egypt and defender of the sun god, Ra. She was also the goddess of pregnancy and childbirth. She was most often depicted as holding an ankh and sistrum. She also helped protect against contagious diseases and evil spirits.

Isis was one of the main characters of the Osiris myth, in which she resurrects her slain brother and husband, the divine king Osiris, and produces and protects his heir, Horus. She was believed to help the dead enter the afterlife as she had helped Osiris, and she was considered the divine mother of the pharaoh. She was usually portrayed in art as a human woman wearing a throne-like hieroglyph on her head.

Hathor was a sky deity, and the consort of the sky god Horus and the sun god Ra. She was one of several goddesses who acted as the Eye of Ra, Ra's feminine counterpart. Her beneficent side represented music, dance, joy and love. More than any other deity, she exemplifies the Egyptian perception of femininity.

Atum was known as the finisher of the world. Atum is one of the most important and frequently mentioned deities from earliest times, as evidenced by his prominence in the Pyramid Texts, where he is portrayed as both a creator and father to the king. Atum was a self-created deity, the first being to emerge from the darkness and endless watery abyss that existed before creation.

Horus was usually depicted as a falcon-headed man, and as a symbol of kingship over the entire kingdom of Egypt. Horus was the son of Isis and Osiris, and he plays a key role in the Osiris myth as Osiris's heir and the rival to Set, the murderer and brother of Osiris.

Anubis was the god of death and Underworld. He was usually depicted as a canine, and of his prominent roles was to usher souls into the afterlife. He attended the weighing scale during the "Weighing of the Heart", in which it was determined whether a soul would be allowed to enter the realm of the dead.

Osiris was considered the god of fertility, agriculture, the afterlife, the dead, resurrection, and vegetation. He was classically depicted as a green-skinned deity with a pharaoh's beard, partially mummy-wrapped at the legs, wearing a distinctive atef crown, and holding a symbolic crook and flail.

Hapi was the god of the annual flooding of the Nile, and one of the four sons of Horus. These floods deposited rich, fertile soil on the river's banks, allowing the Egyptians to grow crops in an area that was otherwise a desert.

Egypt Gods Info Cards

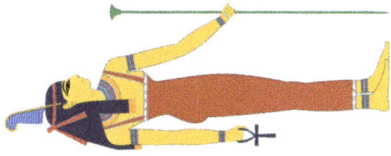

Maat

Amun

Ra

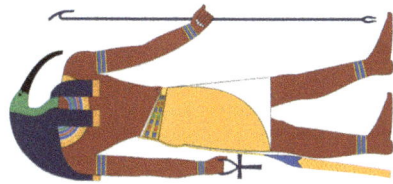

Thoth

Maat was the god of truth, balance, order, harmony, law, morality, and justice. Maat represents the ethical and moral principle that all Egyptian citizens were expected to follow throughout their daily lives. Maat also regulated the stars, seasons, and the actions of mortals and the deities who had brought order from chaos at the moment of creation.

Ra was the god of the sun, order, kings and the sky. Ra was believed to rule in all parts of the created world. Since the people regarded Ra as a principal god, creator of the universe and the source of life, he had a strong influence and considered King of the Gods. He was also the father of Hathor, Bastet and Maat.

Amun was the husband of Amunet and rose to national importance with his fusion with the Sun god, Ra, to become Amun-Ra. He was the champion of the poor or troubled and central to personal piety. He was typically depicted with two plumes on his head, the ankh symbol and the was scepter.

Thoth was often depicted with the head of an ibis. He was the god of the moon, wisdom, writing, hieroglyphs, science, magic, art, and judgment. Thoth played vital roles in maintaining the universe. He was also heavily associated with the arbitration of godly disputes, and the judgment of the dead.

PAPER PLATE SUNDIAL

Instructions

Ancient Egyptians built obelisks which created shadows, forming a kind of sundial, enabling citizens to divide the day in two parts by indicating noon. The oldest known sundial was found in Egypt and dates from the time of Thutmose III, about 1,500 years BC.

Cut a hole in the center of the paper plate with scissors. Glue into plate with craft glue. Allow to dry completely. Mark when you want to "start" the clock and place outside where the sun matches up with that marking. Make sure it is in an area that will receive sunlight all day and not near structures that could create shadows. Continue marking throughout the day on every hour as the shadow moves around the plate. Indicate what time each marking is. Continue until evening. Place outside another day in same location. Do the markings match the correct time?

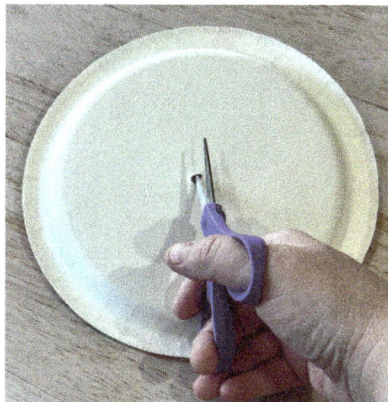

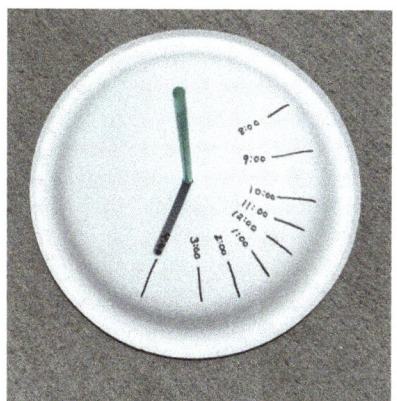

Materials

- Paper Plate
- Scissors
- Straw or Craft Stick
- Craft Glue
- Marker

SENET GAME

Instructions

Senet is considered the oldest board game in the world. The oldest hieroglyphics displaying a Senet game date back to 3100 BC. Senet is a two-game player where each player has 5 pieces. The object of Senet is to be the first player to get all your pieces off the board.

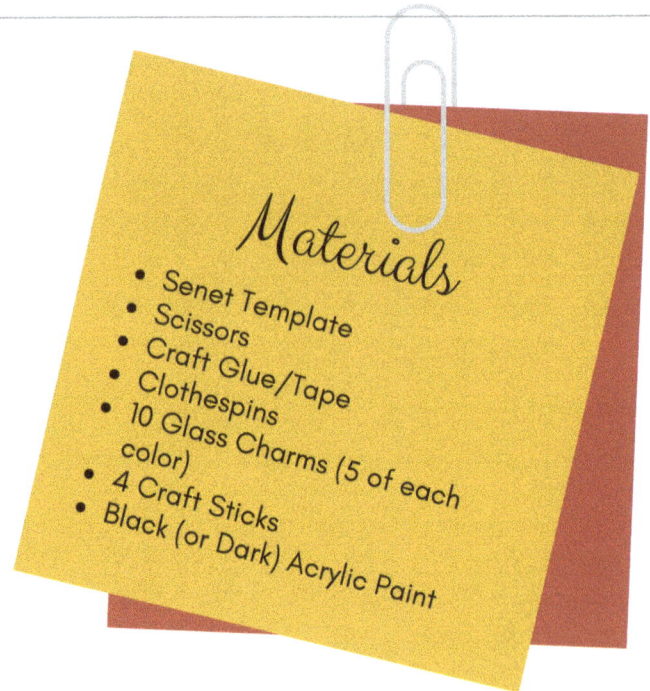

Materials

- Senet Template
- Scissors
- Craft Glue/Tape
- Clothespins
- 10 Glass Charms (5 of each color)
- 4 Craft Sticks
- Black (or Dark) Acrylic Paint

Cut out included Senet template. Fold top piece along lines and glue together as indicated. Allow glue to dry completely. It may be helpful to use clothespins to hold pieces in place as they dry. Glue base piece onto top piece to form a rectangle box. Paint craft sticks black on one side (or another dark color) with acrylic paint.

Provide child with board, painted sticks and 10 charms, five of each color. Use the included Senet rule poster to learn to play the game.

Good luck!

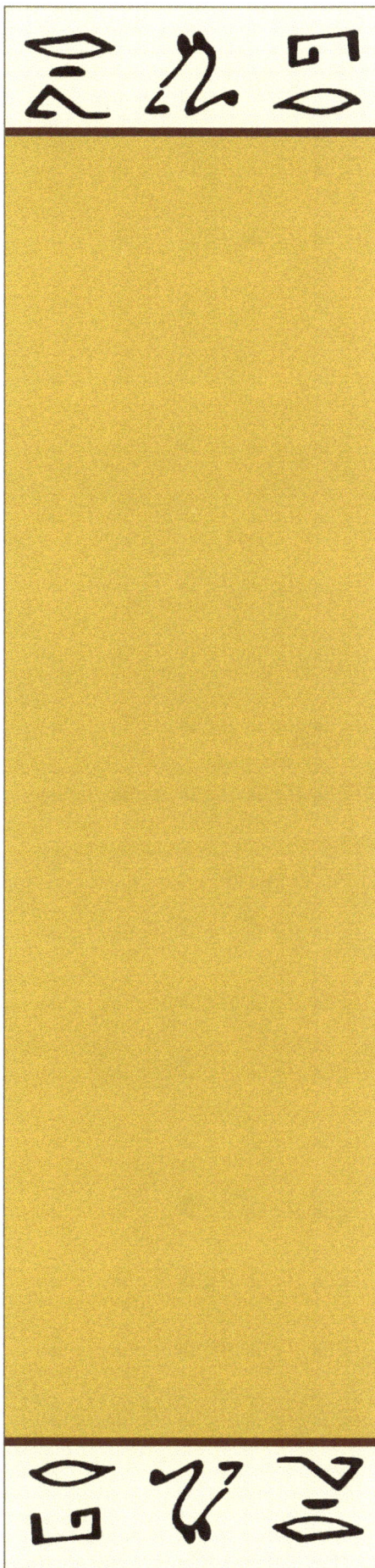

Senet Game

Glue Here

Glue Here

Glue Here

Glue Here

Glue Here

Glue Here

Glue Here

Glue Here

Senet Rules

- **Move through the board** – The board consists of 30 houses or squares. The object is to move through the board, getting all your pieces off the board.
  - **Fill the houses** – At the beginning of the game, you must place your pieces on the first row. Player 1 will place their pieces on the first, third, fifth, seventh, and ninth houses. Player 2 will place their pieces on the second, fourth, sixth, eighth, and tenth houses. *Only one piece can be placed in each house at once.
- **Use senet sticks.** Throw the painted sticks in the air.
  - 3 black & 1 plain = move one house and toss again.
  - 2 black & 2 plain = move two houses and lose a turn.
  - 1 black & 3 plain = move three houses and lose a turn.
  - 4 black = move 5 houses and toss again.
  - 4 plain = move four houses and toss again.
- **Play with five game pieces.** Senet is a two-player game. Each player gets five game pieces and must move all the pieces off the board to win.
- **Capture and protect houses.** Sometimes a house is blocked by another player. If a house occupied by another player, you can capture the piece. The other player's piece will be moved back to the house your piece was on at the beginning of your turn. However, if two or more of another player's pieces are next to each other, that house is protected, and the turn cannot be completed.
- **Picture Houses** – If you land on one of these houses, there are special rules you have to follow:
  - The *House of Second Birth* (15): place that token on square 1, at the start of the game board.
  - The *House of Happiness* (26): all pieces need to pass through this house to win and must land on the house exactly. If you do not roll in such a way that you'll move exactly to this house, you have to stay in place until your next turn.
  - The *House of Water* is marked by three zigzagged lines. If you land on the House of Water, you have to move straight back to the *House of Rebirth*, which is marked by three sideways stick figures.
  - The *House of Three Truths* (27): you can throw your sticks again. If you get three plain sides up, you can automatically remove this piece from the board.
  - The *House of Two Judges* (29): throw your sticks again. If you get two plain sticks, you can remove your piece from the board.
  - The *House of Horus* (30): you must toss your sticks again. You cannot remove your piece until you toss your sticks and only one colored stick is facing upwards.

● 1	○ 2	● 3	○ 4	● 5	○ 6	● 7	○ 8	● 9	○ 10
20	19	18	17	16	15	14	13	12	11
21	22	23	24	25	26	27	28	29	30

PAPYRUS MAKING

Instructions

Ancient Egyptians made papyrus paper by arranging two layers of papyrus, one atop the other, at right angles. The layers are then pressed together, and the gum released by the breakdown of the plant's cellular structure acts as a glue which bonds the sheet together. Examples of surviving papyrus paper are as old as 2500 BC, about the time the pyramids were built!

Materials

- Kraft Paper
- Scissors
- Craft Stick Glue
- Black Marker (Optional)

Cut out craft paper into strips forming a rectangle base. Coat a strip with glue stick (or craft glue) and lay perpendicular to the first layer to form the paper. Continue upwards to create a strong base. Make sure each piece has adequate glue to hold together. Continue until strips are used up or sheet is of desired size. Add hieroglyphic illustrations using a black or dark colored marker (optional) using the included hieroglyphic alphabet sheet.

Discuss: How does this type of paper differ from paper today? What is different? What is the same?

Hieroglyphics Equivalents

A B C D E F G H I
J K L M N O P Q R
S T U V W X Y Z

Hieroglyphics Code Cards

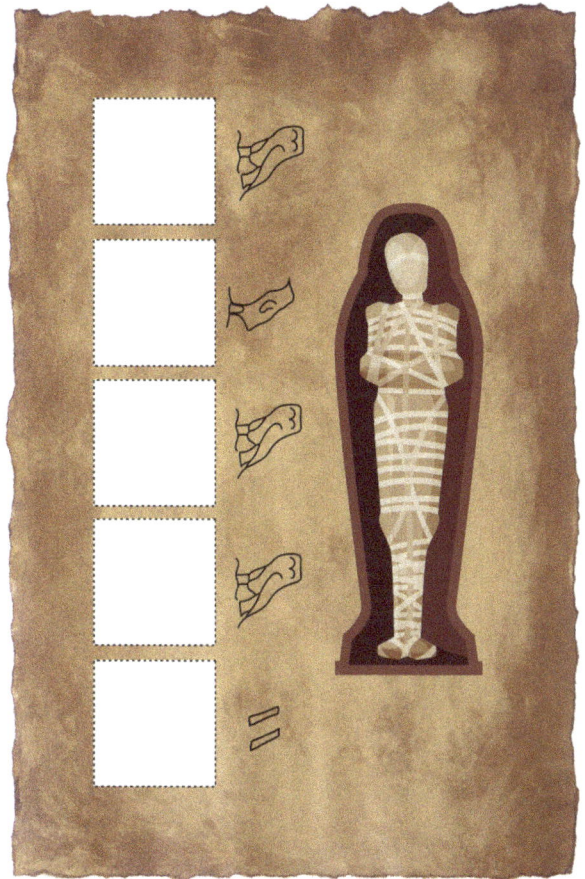

Hieroglyphics Code Cards

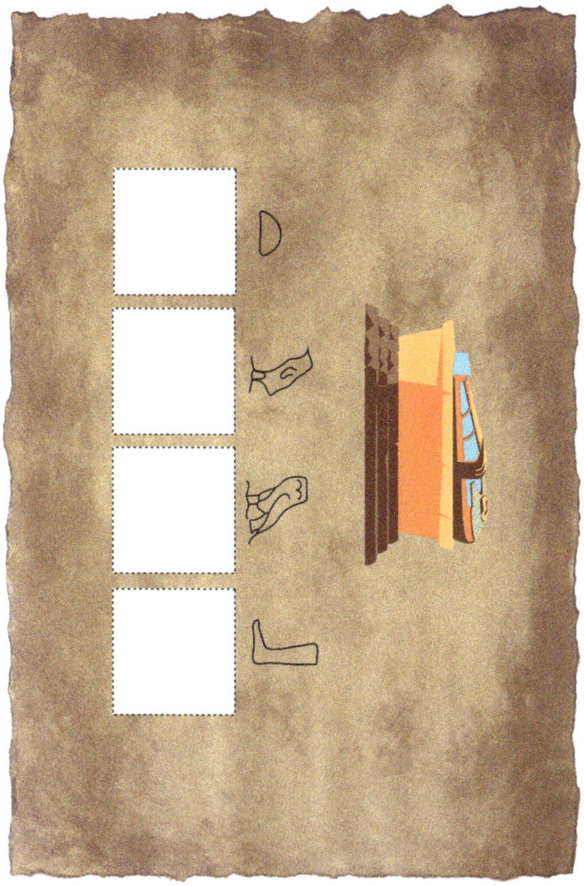

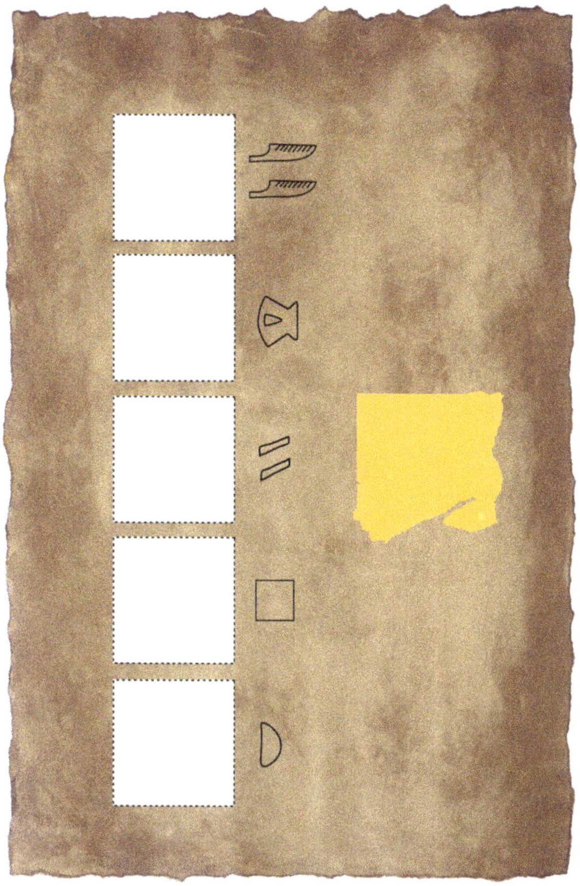

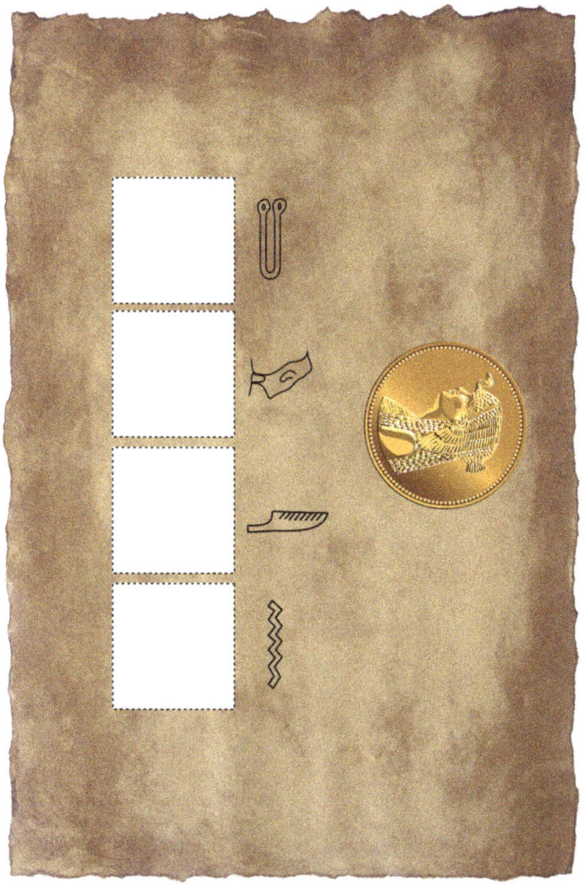

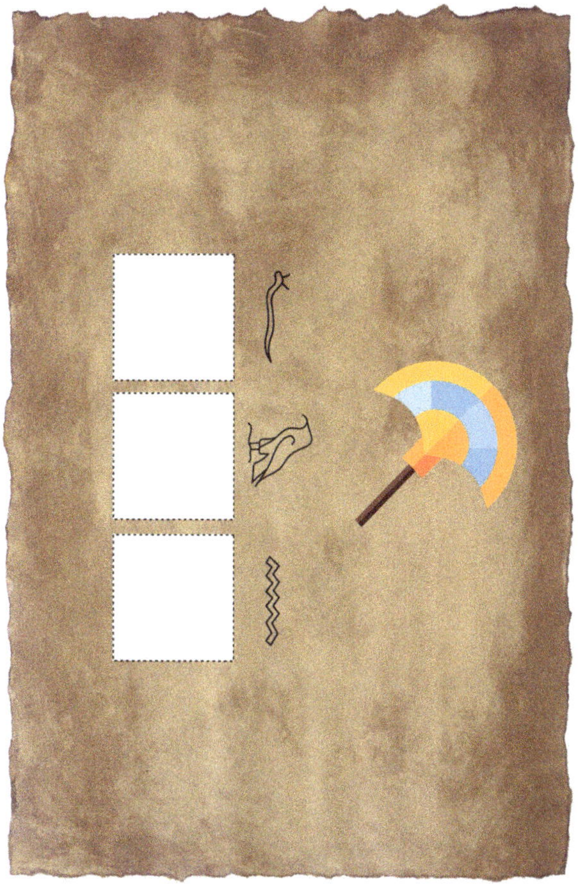

Hieroglyphics Code Cards

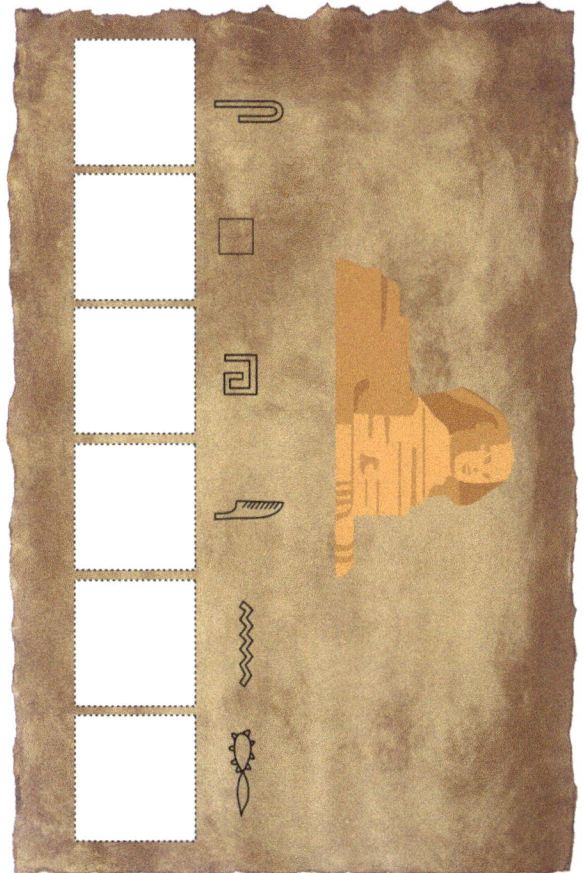

Hieroglyphics Code Cards

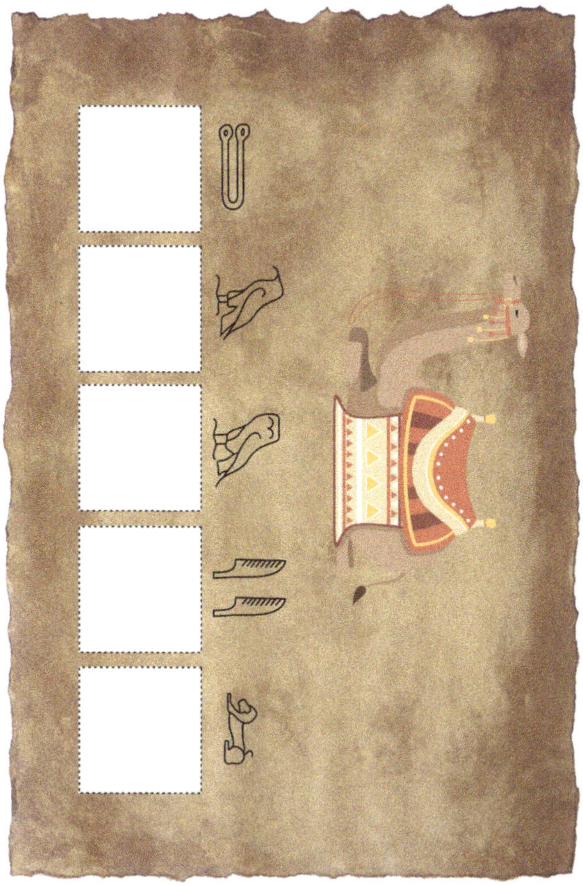

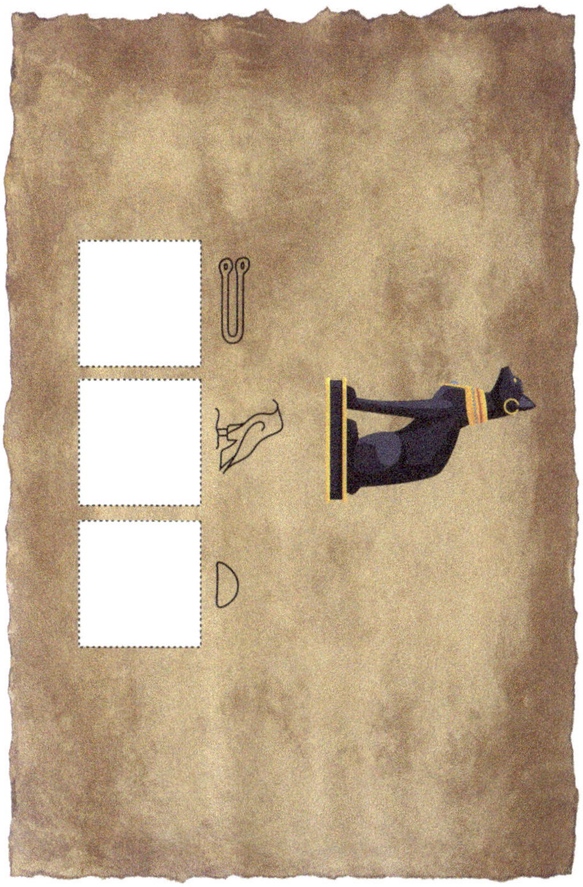

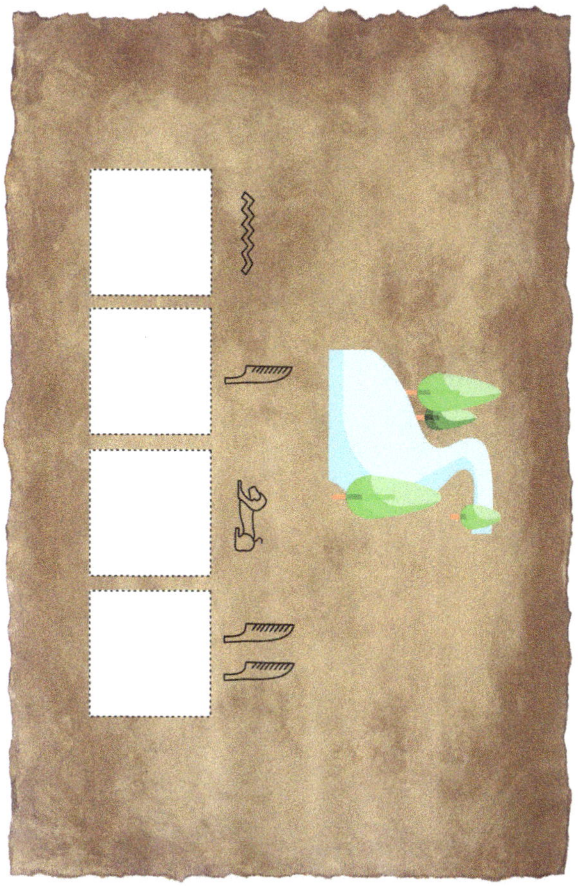

Hieroglyphics Code Cards

A	A	A	A	A	A	A	A	A
A	B	B	B	C	C	C	C	C
C	D	D	E	E	E	E	E	E
E	E	F	F	G	G	H	H	I
I	I	I	J	J	K	K	K	K
L	L	L	M	M	M	M	M	M
M	N	N	N	N	N	N	N	N
O	O	O	O	O	P	P	P	Q
R	R	R	S	S	S	S	S	S
T	T	T	T	U	U	V	W	X
X	Y	Y	Y	Y	Z			

TALE OF THE DOOMED PRINCE

There lived an old crocodile in this lake, and when the prince ran into the water, the crocodile grabbed the prince and said, "I am your fate." He dragged the prince to an island. When they arrived, he told the prince, "There is only one way in which you can escape your fate. You must do me a favor. A wicked prince rules this lake. If you can help me defeat him, I will let you go."

9

The night after the child was born, the seven stars of the goddess Hathor twinkled brightly in the sky. In the morning, they came down to earth in the form of seven sacred cows. The pharaoh and his queen showed them their new baby. They predicted that the new prince would die by one of three dooms – a crocodile, snake or dog.

2

Once upon a time, an ancient Egyptian Pharaoh had everything a Pharaoh could desire; everything except for one thing: a child. The pharaoh prayed to gods every day, asking them to bless him with a son. A few months later, his queen became pregnant and had a baby boy.

1

So the prince helped the old crocodile and together they fought the wicked prince and defeated him. The old crocodile told the young prince, "I will keep my promise as you have done me this favor." The young prince was overjoyed after facing each of his dooms and overcoming each one. He went home to his princess, who thought her husband was dead. She was overjoyed to see her prince again, and the two lived happily ever after.

THE END.

10

The pharaoh, afraid for his son's safety, built a special palace, way up high in the mountains, to protect his son from the awful dooms. For a few years, all was well and the young prince had a relatively peaceful childhood.

3

A few years later, the prince was out hunting with his dog, and his beloved dog looked at him and snarled: "I am your fate." The prince started to run, and the dog ran after him. Although the prince could run faster than almost anyone, he was not as speedy as his dog. He knew his dog hated water, and so he ran into a lake.

8

One night, as the prince lay sleeping, the princess lay awake. As the moonlight was shining through the window, and she saw a snake slowly slithering across the floor. The princess quickly called the guard and was able to kill the snake before it harmed the prince. The princess was very pleased that she had saved her husband from at least one doom.

7

One day, the prince sees a man with a dog outside his palace window. He asks his father, the pharaoh, for a dog. The pharaoh remembers the prediction, but the young prince is very persistent, so eventually he is given a dog.

4

Assembly Instructions

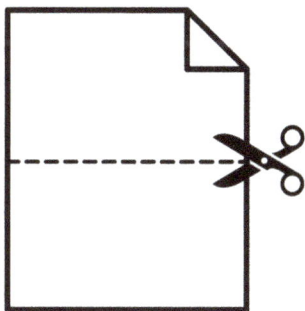

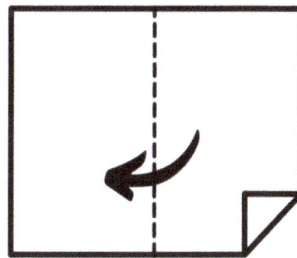

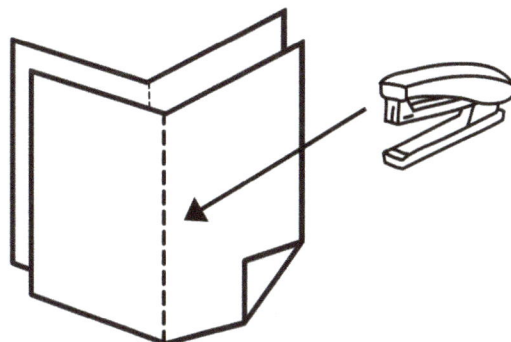

Cut paper in half on lines. Fold each page of book as indicated. Collate together so pages match up appropriately. Staple spine to hold together.

Over the years, the child becomes a handsome prince. He decided to leave his protective palace and travel to Nahrin to face his doom. He found a young princess locked in a tower and wins her heart by leaping to her room, rescuing her from her captivity. The princess' father approves of the young prince and the two are married.

5

Soon after marrying the princess, the young prince tells the princess about the three dooms. The princess becomes worried about his dog and urged the prince to get rid of the dog. "No!" cried the prince. "We've grown up together. I would never do such a thing."
His wife knew she couldn't change his mind, so she watched closely over him from that day on.

6

Egyptian Currency

The pound is the main unit of Egyptian currency. One pound is divided into one hundred piastres.

Egyptian Currency

The pound is the main unit of Egyptian currency. One pound is divided into one hundred piastres.

Ancient gold stater of Nectanebo II: reverse with hieroglyphs

Egyptian Currency

The pound is the main unit of Egyptian currency. One pound is divided into one hundred piastres.

*This is just a sample of some of the currency currently in circulation. Please note that some of the money depicted may be larger or smaller in reality and these pages only include one side in order to adhere to legal requirements regarding currency reproduction for educational and artistic use.

Ancient Egyptian Music

Double Oboe

Sistrum

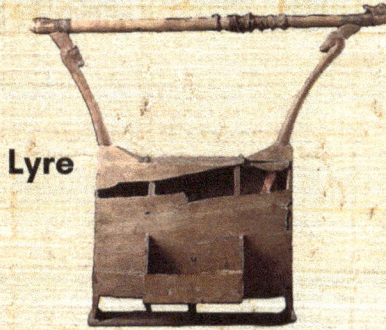

Lyre

Lyre

Long Lute

Standing Harp

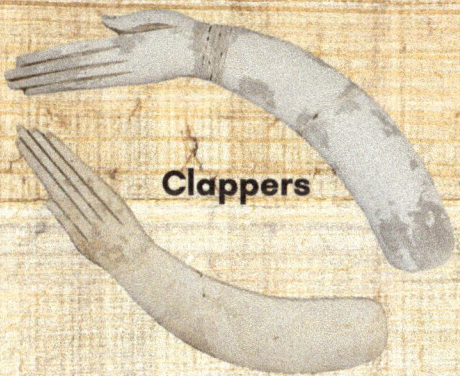

Clappers

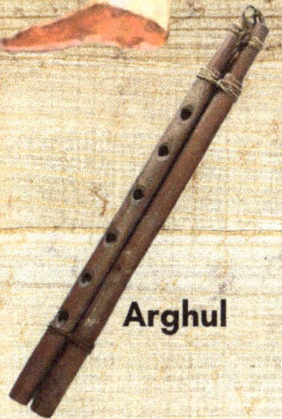

Arghul

Drum

Painted Harp

Dancers

Units of Measurement

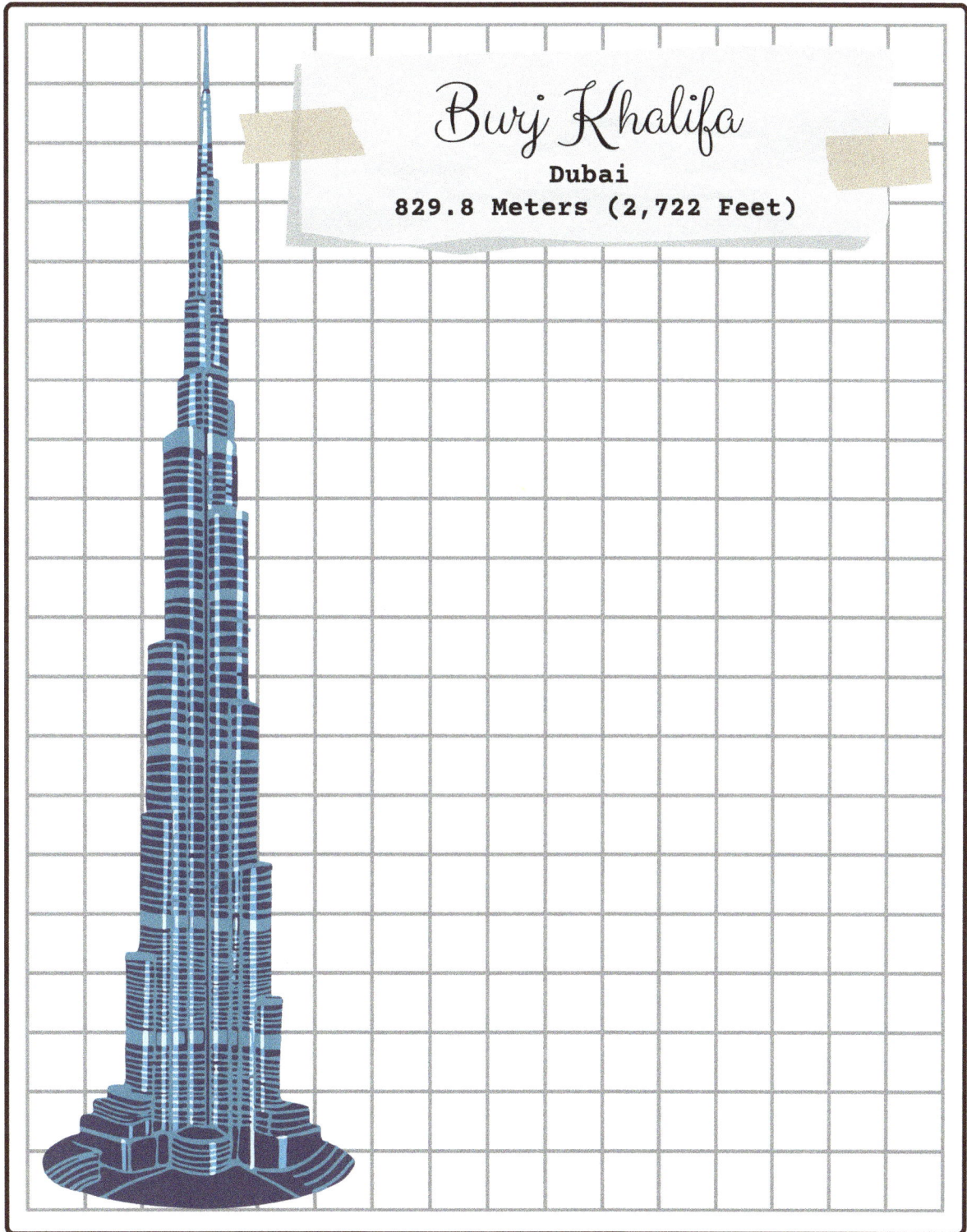

Burj Khalifa
Dubai
829.8 Meters (2,722 Feet)

Units of Measurement

Eiffel Tower
France
330 Meters (1,083 Feet)

Great Pyramid
Egypt
137 Meters (448 Feet)

Big Ben
England
96 Meters (315 Feet)

Units of Measurement

Statute of Liberty
United States
93 Meters (305 Feet)

Taj Mahal
India
73 Meters (240 Feet)

Sydney Opera House
Australia
65 Meters (213 Feet)

Colosseum
Italy
48 Meters (157 Feet)

Units of Measurement

Christ the Redeemer
Brazil
38 Meters (125 Feet)

Parthenon
Greece
14 Meters (45 Feet)

19
18
17
16
15
14
13
12
11
10
9
8
7
6
5
4
3
2
1

The tallest building in the world is Burj Khalifa, located in Dubai, United Arab Emirates. Measuring a total height of 829.8 m (2,722 ft) (just over half a mile), the Burj Khalifa has been the tallest structure and building in the world since its topping out in 2009, supplanting Taipei 101, the previous holder of that status.

Use the included ruler to measure the height of the different world landmarks. Identify how many units of measurement each is. Compare to the other buildings. Which is the tallest? Which is the shortest? Put them in order of height. Which structures surprise you with their height?

Life Cycle Spinner

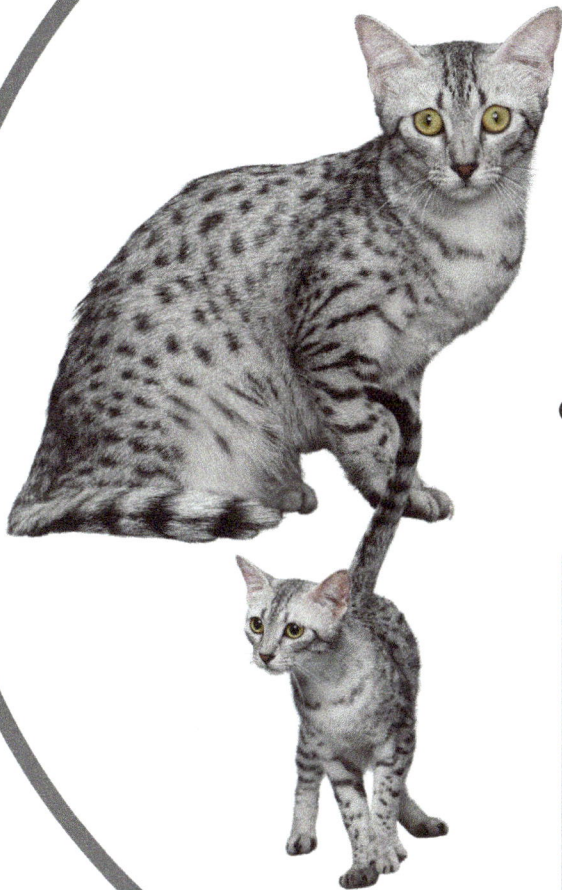

Life Cycle
of the
Egyptian
Mau

hind leg	head
ear	tail
back	

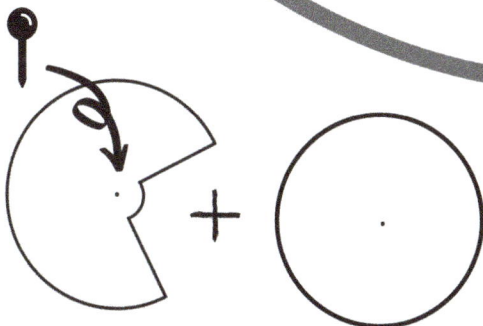

adolecent

kitten

adult

pregnant

| eye | nose | whiskers | mouth |
| chest | fore leg | paw | belly |

Parts of an Egyptian Mau

eye

nose

whiskers

mouth

chest

fore leg

paw

ear

head

back

tail

belly

hind leg

Parts of an Egyptian Mau

Learning to Write

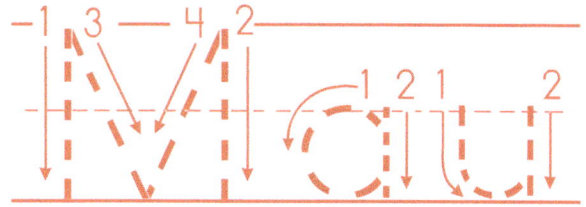

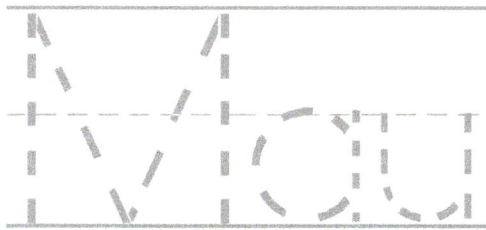

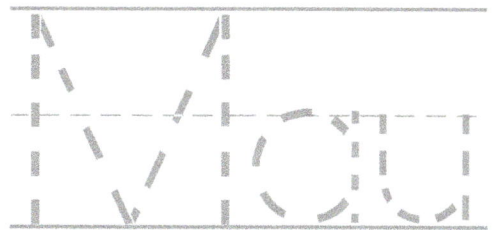

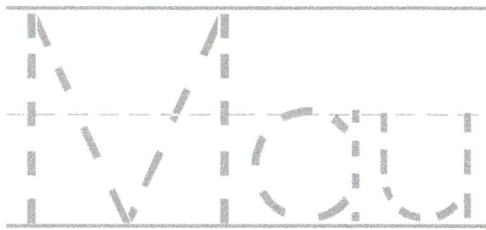

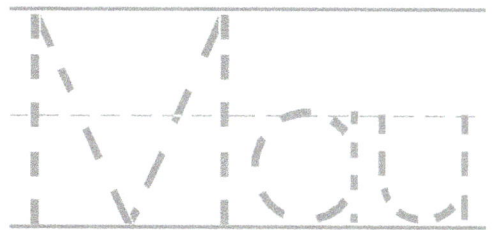

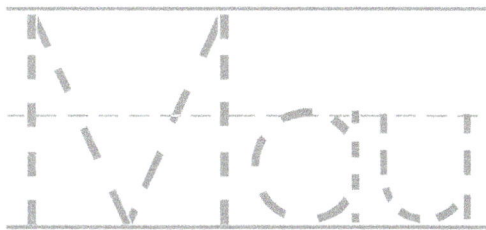

Mau

KHAYAMIYA FABRIC

Instructions

Khayamiya is a type of decorative appliqué textile historically used to decorate tents across the Middle East. Today, they are primarily made in Cairo, Egypt, along what is known as the Street of the Tentmakers. Khayamiya are colorful, elaborately patterned appliqués applied to the interior of tents, serving a dual function of shelter and ornament.

Use included design to trace pattern onto thick, light-colored fabric. Linens and canvas work well for this. Lay a sheet of carbon paper face down onto fabric and place pattern on top. A clipboard helps keep the pattern from shifting. Trace around each design detail. It may be helpful to use a colored pencil so completed lines are indicated. Use colored markers to color in completed fabric in bright colors.

Display the completed textile.

Khayamiya Design

STEPPE EAGLE CRAFT

Instructions

The steppe eagle, *Aquila nipalensis*, is a large bird of prey, and the national bird of Egypt. Like all eagles, it belongs to the family Accipitridae and is mainly dark brown in color with a long, thick neck and a relatively small head in comparison to the rest of the body. Their total length can range from 60 to 89 cm (24 to 35 in) in fully-grown adults.

Have the child color the included steppe eagle template, focusing on the beak, eyes and central face. Cut out the eagle circle and add glue onto the outer edge of the illustration. Adhere feathers in a circle around the outer edge onto glue. Repeat laying feathers inward until the illustration has been filled with feathers. Use multiple variations of brown feathers for a realistic look. Allow to dry thoroughly.

Compare to photo of an adult steppe eagle - how does the art version compare?

Steppe Eagle Craft

FEZ HAT

Instructions

The fez (or tarboush) has a complicated history in Egypt. The fez is a felt headdress, usually red, with a tassel attached to the top, and was once the mark of the elite in Egypt, signifying power and status for the wearer. Today they are rarely made in Egypt, as they are now considered politically incorrect, due to their ties with the Ottoman Empire. However, they remain an icon of Egyptian history.

Cut out hat from template as indicated with red felt. Sew (or glue) the circle piece to both the side pieces, as indicated. Trim and adjust as necessary for a comfortable fit. Sew or glue the sides together to complete the hat base. It may be necessary to measure child's head several times. Cut several lengths of black yarn using included pattern. Fold over the yarn and tie securely about 1" from to (2-3 cm). Sew or glue black tassel to the top.

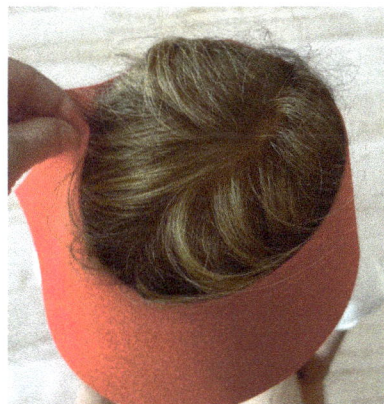

Fez Hat Pattern

Older Children

Younger Children

Cut one of red felt

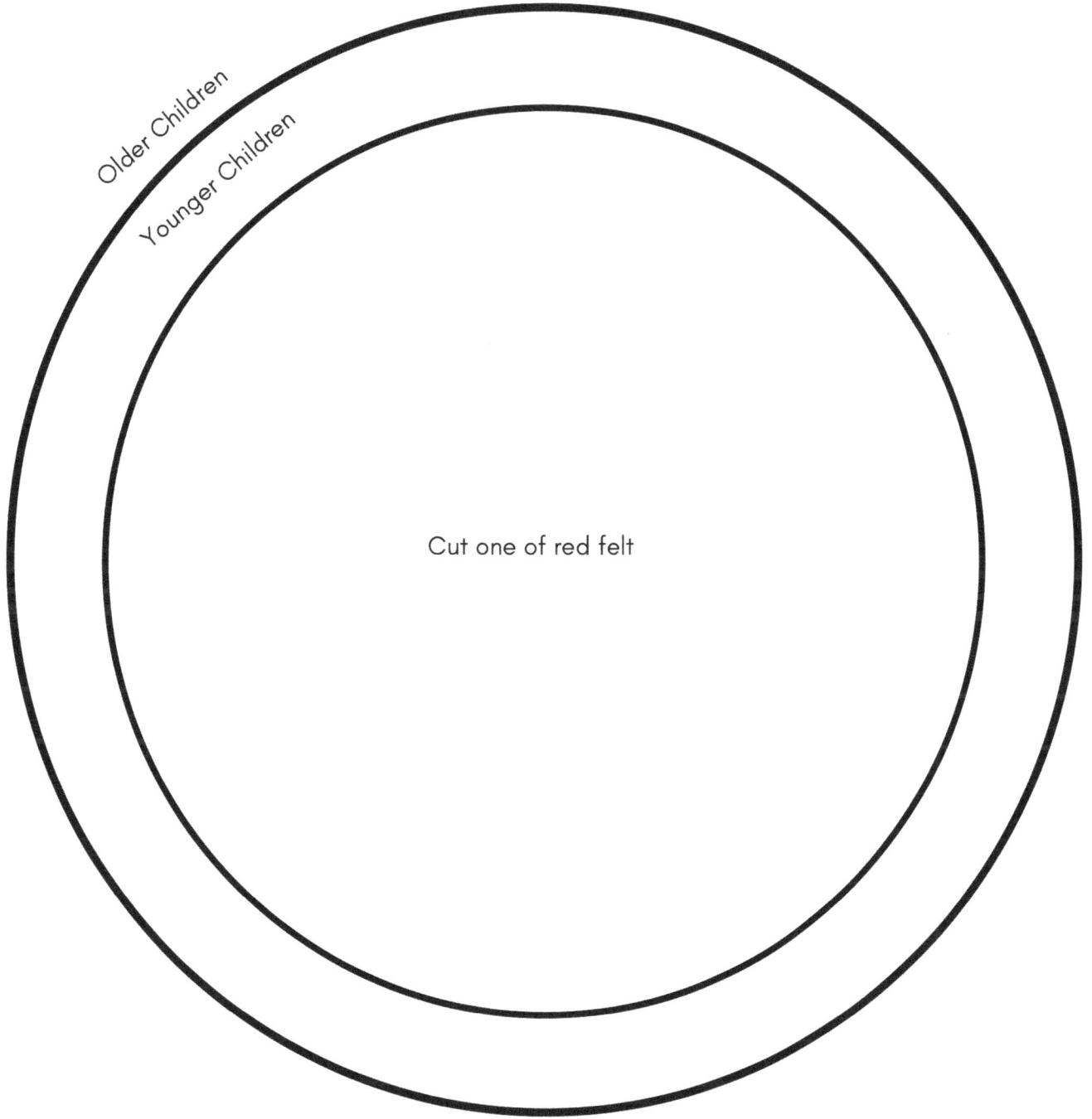

Cut on fold if available

Cut two of red felt (or cut one on fold)

Cut black yarn this length

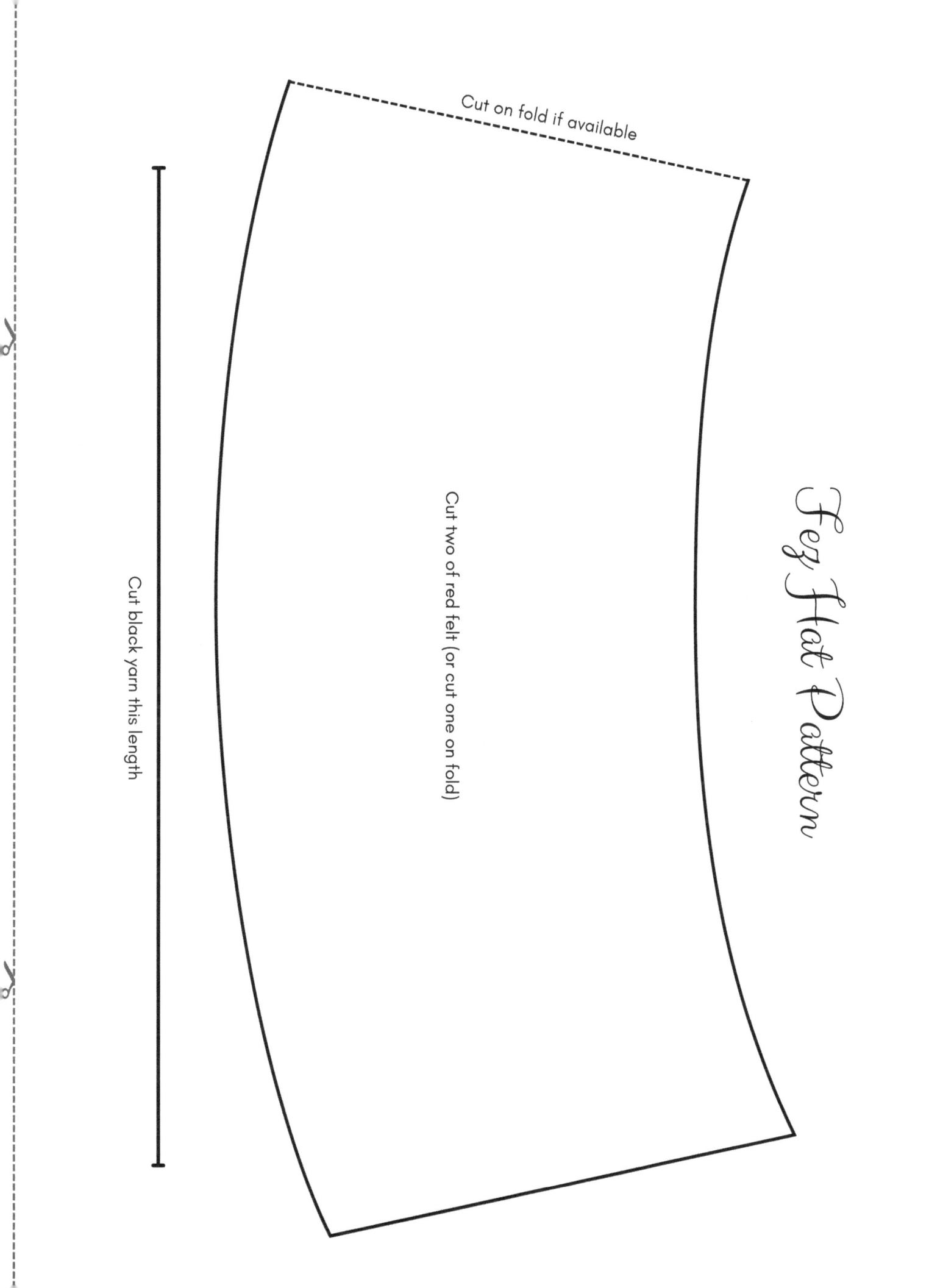

Fez Hat Pattern

FANOUS LANTERN

Instructions

During the month of Ramadan, lanterns (known as fanous in Arabic) are used as both decoration and as a source of light, especially in Egypt. The Fanous has become a worldwide symbol for well over a thousand years. In modern day, with the availability of electricity and technology, lanterns are not really needed as a source of light. Instead, the Fanous is used as decoration for popular Ramadan tents, gatherings, and city streets to create a more festive ambiance during the holy month of Ramadan.

Materials
- Fanous Lantern Template
- Construction Paper
- Craft Knife
- Crayons or Markers
- Scissors
- Craft Glue
- Flameless Light

Use included Fanous lantern template as a pattern over construction paper and cut out using a craft knife - make sure to have adult supervision/assistance for this step. Or alternatively, color template to make a unique, colorful design. Fold as indicated and use glue stick to adhere sides together. Fold over the bottom tabs to create base. Punch holes as indicated. Place a flameless candle or LED light into the bottom of the lantern. Make several lanterns of various colors and several on a string - Happy Ramadan!

Ramadan Lantern

PILLARS OF ISLAM CRAFT

Instructions

About one fifth of the world's population is Muslim, a belief system based on the Qur'an and the teachings of Muhammad. Egypt has approximately 90% Muslim believers. Islam has five major belief pillars which constitute the basic norms of Islamic practice. They include: the declaration of faith (shahada), prayer (salah), almsgiving or charity (zakat), fasting (sawm) and pilgrimage (hajj). They are accepted by all Muslims irrespective of ethnic, regional or sectarian differences.

Color in the included pillars assorted colors. Cut out and glue each of the five different standards of belief into each of the pillar's center. Cut out the pillars and glue onto colored construction paper. Allow to dry completely and display.

Discuss: How do the pillars of Islam differ from the standards of your belief system (if different)? How are they similar?

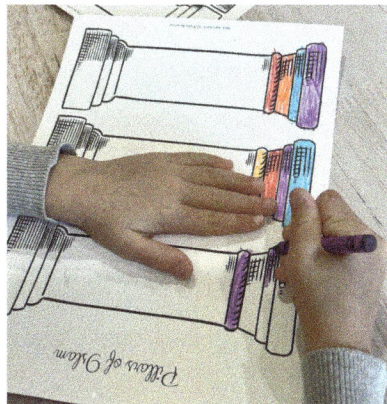

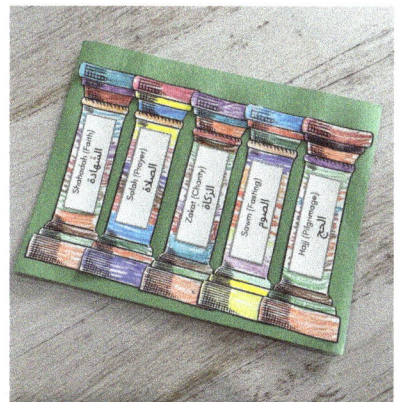

Materials

- Pillars of Islam Template
- Colored Construction Paper
- Crayons or Markers
- Scissors
- Glue Stick

Pillars of Islam

Shahadah (Faith) الشَهادة	Salah (Prayer) الصلاة

Zakat (Charity) الزكاة	Sawm (Fasting) الصوم

Hajj (Pilgrimage) الحج

Pillars of Islam

HAMSA HAND INCENSE BURNER

Instructions

Egypt has a long-standing history of burning incense, with the harmonious, thick scents being used in the worship of their gods. Resins and woods were burned daily at temples, each scent representing meaning, ceremony, and purpose. The hamsa (خمسة) is a palm-shaped amulet popular throughout North Africa and in the Middle East.

Materials

- Craft Clay
- Rolling Pin
- Craft Stick
- Bronze or Gold Paint
- Incense Cones
- Lighter/Matches

Flatten the craft clay with a rolling pin to about 8-10mm or a little over 1/4" thickness. Lay the child's hand on the clay and trace around it with a craft stick. After removing the hand, cut scrap away the balance of the clay with the craft stick until only the hand remains. Trace onto the hand print the Eye of Horus (illustration below), a symbol of well-being, healing, and protection. Add additional design elements as desired. Place the clay hand into a curved bowl and allow to dry several days until completely dry and hard. Paint the hand with bronze or gold paint. Allow to dry completely. Place an incense cone into the center of the hand and light with a lighter or matches - make sure to have adult supervision for this step!

COTTON CRAFT

Instructions

Egyptian cotton (*Gossypium barbadense*) is associated with quality and superior softness. It is one of several species of cotton cultivated and used around the world. Egyptian cotton has particularly long fibers and is ironically found more commonly in South America. It was brought to "fame" in the 1800s by a Frenchman, Monsieur Jumel, who was living in Cairo. Soon this species of cotton became associated with luxury, and Egypt became a major exporter for this highly desired cotton.

Materials

- Cotton Craft Template
- Cotton Balls
- Craft Glue

Use the included cotton craft template and provide child with craft glue and cotton balls. Have child glue the cotton pieces into the bur (supporting structure that houses the cotton boil). Continue until the cotton plant is full of cotton balls. Compare and contrast the different types of cotton with the included info cards - how do the different species differ in appearance?

Cotton Craft

Cotton Species Cards

MOST POPULAR

Upland Cotton
Gossypium hirsutum

Egyptian Cotton
Gossypium barbadense

Tree Cotton
Gossypium arboreum

Levant Cotton
Gossypium herbaceum

FUL MEDAMES

ingredients

- 2 - 14 ounces can fava beans
- 1 - 15 ounces canned chickpeas
- 1 teaspoon cumin
- ½ teaspoon Kosher salt

Sauce:

- ½ cup extra virgin olive oil
- ¼ cup lemon juice
- 4 garlic cloves, crushed
- 1 tablespoon green chilis
- Salt and pepper to taste
- Fresh parsley
- Hardboiled egg

directions

- Pour the fava beans and chickpeas into a colander to drain. Rinse beans with cold water.
- Transfer the rinsed, drained beans to a medium saucepan over medium heat, and add 1 and half cups of cold water. Add cumin and kosher salt.
- Bring mixture to a boil, then reduce heat to low and let simmer uncovered for 20 minutes or most of the water is absorbed. Crush beans during mixing to get desired consistency.
- Combine all the ingredients for the sauce in a small bowl and serve over the bean mixture.
- Serve with fresh parsley and hardboiled eggs.

Adult Supervision Required

Ful Medames

INGREDIENTS

FAVA BEANS

CHICKPEAS

CUMIN

KOASHER SALT

EXTRA VIRGIN OLIVE OIL

LEMON JUICE

GARLIC

GREEN CHILIS

SALT/PEPPER

PARSLEY

HARDBOILED EGG

The Sahara Desert

Sahara Desert Habitat Matching

Cut out circles of animals and match into appropriate habitat on Sahara scene.

Steppe Eagle

Ibex

Gazelle

Horse

Viper

Fennec fox

Jackel

Chameleon

Cape Hare

Jerboa

Desert Hedgehog

Lizard

Camel

Barbary Sheep

Crocodile

Ostrich

Monitor

Cobra

Scorpion

Features of the Sahara

Climate

The Sahara is dominated by two climatic regimes: a dry subtropical climate in the north and a dry tropical climate in the south.

Flora

Due to the lack of water, plant life is relatively scarce in the Sahara, with most found near water sources. Date palm trees and African peyote cactus may be found as well as scattered concentrations of grasses and shrubs.

Fauna

The Sahara has over 70 species of mammals, 90 species of resident birds, 100 species of reptiles, and numerous species of arthropods, all of which has adapted to the hyper-arid conditions, fierce winds, intense heat and wide temperature swings.

Water

Water is scarce in the Sahara, but it does contain two permanent rivers, the Nile and the Niger, as well as 20+ seasonal lakes and aquifers, which are the primary sources of water for more than 90 major oases in the desert.

KOLLA POTTERY PAINTING

Instructions

Egyptian artistic painted pottery vessel known as "kolla" are made of clay and painted bright colors. Egyptian pottery dates back thousands of years into the history of the Ancient Egyptians. Today, this handmade colorful pottery is available along the streets of many tourist locations.

Provide child with terracotta pots and paint with acrylic paints. Make sure to cover any areas that could be damaged by paints. Egg cartons make good containers to hold a variety of paint colors. Use various colors to create bold and detailed designs. Use the included matching cards as inspiration. Younger children may need additional assistance. Allow to dry completely. Use included matching cards to compare designs.

Materials

- Mini Terracotta Pots
- Acrylic Paints, Assorted Colors
- Paint Brush(es)

Kolla Pottery Matching

Kolla Pottery Matching

Egyptian Arabic Language Cards

سلام عليكم

salaam 'aleikum

Hello

مع سلامة

ma'a salaameh

Goodbye

لو سمحت

law samaHt

Pardon Me

شكرا

shukran

Thanks

Egyptian Arabic Language Cards

بكم دة

bikam dah?

How Much Is This?

اخبارك ايه؟

akhbaarak eh?

How's It Going?

انا عيز

ana 3ayiiz…

I want...

اية دة من فضلك

eh dah min faDlak?

What's This, Please?

Savy Activities

Travel the world through the interactive learning activities of **Savy Activities**; these hands-on resources provide parents, caregivers and educators practical ways to teach children about the world around them. Each book features a country, location or time period where subjects such as geography, history, vocabulary, reading, language, science, mathematics, music and art come alive by engaging auditory, visual and kinesthetic learning styles.

All activity books include geography with applicable maps, landmarks and locations. Historical events and time periods are visually represented with full color posters and flashcards, if applicable. Each book includes a set of fun-fact cards, poster and flag, if applicable. Paper models allow children to create 3D creations of major landmarks and structures. All books include a life cycle and anatomy of a plant, animal or organic compound, with flashcards and 3-part cards featuring important structures applicable to the theme.

Children learn scientific principles through active experiments and activities. Traditional customs, festivals, toys, clothing and art are also explored. Each book includes an exclusive themed mini-story featuring historical events or traditional mythology and folklore to promote vocabulary and reading. Where applicable, world languages are introduced through engaging flashcards, posters and tracing work. Each country has been meticulously researched by interviewing native persons and/or personal travel experiences to ensure the authentic culture is fully explored.

Savy Activities utilizes concepts from multiple educational methods to create unique resources allowing children a tangible and enjoyable way to explore their world. The **Savy Activities** series should not be viewed as a curriculum, but rather complimentary thematic resources to enhance traditional education. Because the individual needs and knowledge of children varies within standardized grade levels, **Savy Activities** resources have the flexibility to be used with preschool learners through early to mid-elementary years. For younger learners, adult supervision and/or assistance may be needed and activities presented in a simplified version. For older learners, resources may be paired with additional content from other materials to meet learning outcomes.

Check out our other products and resources at **www.SavyActivities.com**

www.ingramcontent.com/pod-product-compliance
Lightning Source LLC
Chambersburg PA
CBHW061220270326
41926CB00032B/4788